BOOKS BY DAVID BRANDT

IS THAT ALL THERE IS?
OVERCOMING DISAPPOINTMENT IN AN AGE OF
DIMINISHED EXPECTATIONS

DON'T STOP NOW, YOU'RE KILLING ME
THE SADOMASOCHISM GAME IN EVERYDAY LIFE
AND HOW NOT TO PLAY IT

DON'T STOP NOW, YOU'RE KILLING ME

The Sadomasochism Game in Everyday Life and How Not to Play It

Dr. David Brandt

POSEIDON PRESS · NEW YORK

10   9   8   7   6   5   4   3   2   1

Library of Congress Cataloging in Publication Data

Brandt, David.
Don't stop now, you're Killing me.

1. Control (Psychology)   2. Psychological games.
3. Sadism.   4. Masochism.   I. Title.
BF632.5.B7   1986   155.2′32   86–5103

ISBN: 0-671-52795-9

The author gratefully acknowledges permission to reprint the following excerpts from previously published material:

PAGE 179 and 189: from *A Psychiatrist's World, The Selected Papers of Karl Menninger, M.D.* Copyright 1939, renewed © 1966 by Karl Menninger. Reprinted by permission of Viking Penguin, Inc.

PAGE 24: from *Masochism in Modern Man.* Copyright 1941 by Theodore Reik. Reprinted by permission of Farrar, Straus and Giroux, Inc.

PAGE 179: from *Assorted Prose.* Copyright by John Updike. Reprinted by permission of Alfred A. Knopf, Inc.

PAGE 173: from *The Language of the Body.* Copyright 1971 by Alexander Lowen. Reprinted by permission of Grune & Stratton, Inc.

PAGE 184: from *Anatomy of Human Destructiveness.* Copyright 1973 by Erich Fromm. Reprinted by permission of Henry Holt and Co.

Acknowledgments

Writing a contemporary psychology book is a bit like dealing in precious gems. First you must "discover" the stone in which it is hidden, then cut it to size and shape, polish it to a brilliant luster, and, finally, sell it. In this multifaceted business, help is more than appreciated, it is absolutely necessary. And as anyone will tell you, good help is hard to come by.

To those who aided me in the task of finding, cutting, polishing, and selling I offer my deep gratitude. Specifically, I want to thank the following people: Sheryl Seacat and Jean Arnold, who offered thoughtful and useful comments on the manuscript; John White, whose excellent consultation on the assessment tools was invaluable; Russell Fuller for his syntactical wizardry and special brand of creativity; Stanley Brandt, Ida Brandt, Robert Brandt, and Joan Swerdlow Brandt for their practical contribution to the research; Bob Kriegel, who was willing to sort out and try on ideas anytime, night or day; Victoria Galland who is truly the master of the one-liner; Harvey Klinger for representing my interests like a brother; Ann Patty, my editor, and her assistant, Michael Sanders, for improving the text and with their good faith making the editing task almost bearable.

I offer a special thanks to my life partner, Laurie Brandt, who was always there, not with coffee and doughnuts, but with the kind of help that only an equal can give. Her knowledge of the material and her readiness to engage in the struggle for expression with me were great blessings. Her contributions to the character and ideas in this book are significant.

Finally, I want to thank my daughter, Kate, who gave me reason to smile even on mornings when I faced a long day of rewriting ahead.

To my parents:
My mother who gave me the will;
My father who gave me the heart.

Contents

Chapter 8
The Making of an Everyday Masochist   179

Chapter 9
Getting into the Change Frame   201

DON'T STOP NOW, YOU'RE KILLING ME

Introduction

Several years ago, two things happened that changed the immediate course of my life. Each was eventful in its own right, but taken together they constituted a remarkable and enigmatic set of circumstances. One was an experience of sheer joy and excitement; the other was overwhelmingly painful.

I had just returned to my office when the phone rang. It was my agent calling from New York with some news on a book proposal I had sent to him only ten days earlier. I was not expecting very much. Several of my psychologist friends had spent years trying unsuccessfully to interest a publisher in their ideas, and I anticipated a rough road ahead. But the news was good. So good, in fact, that I leapt into the air with unbridled joy. The book had been bought by a major publishing house only a week or so after it had left my hands. Heart beating fast, I bounded down the stairs to tell my wife in the office below. Like an excited marsupial I took five steps at a time, but lacking its natural grace I missed the fifth step and went hurtling to the ground.

The pain was excruciating. I knew immediately the damage was extensive, yet I could not accept what had happened. My ankle was not seriously hurt. Or was it? There I was lying on the carpet in agony when moments before I had been celebrating one of the highest moments in my professional life.

Slowly I dragged myself to the refrigerator nearby, wrapped my foot in ice, and reflected on the experience.

Why had this happened? How could I have been so clumsy? Was my unconscious telling me something, or was this merely a freak accident? I found my wife and told her of my great success. She looked first at my wincing face, then down at my pulsating, bluish melon of an ankle, and didn't know whether to laugh or cry. The absurdity of it all struck us at the same time and we collapsed in each other's arms, tears running down our faces.

Later, when I had recovered from that psychodrama, I spent a long time wondering. As a psychologist, I knew that the synchronism of these two events was more than coincidence. I had essentially obliterated a moment of glory, yet consciously I was not aware of my motivation. To allay my confusion I did what I have advised so many of my patients to do. I replayed the experience in my mind to see what my intuition, body, and feelings had to tell me.

I visualized myself on the telephone and felt the sense of joy and delight that accompanied the good news. But I also felt a surge of anxiety. Could I really produce the book I had promised? And could I do it in the time frame stipulated by contract? I had real doubts about my competence. I sensed that a part of me was genuinely uncomfortable with my good fortune and actually entertained the thought (oh, so briefly) that such glad tidings would have to be followed by an equal quantity of bad luck. I felt overwhelmed by these strong, contradictory feelings, and as I ran down the stairs I was emotionally off balance. That was all it took for me to fall. A small misstep and the rest was, as they say, history.

Such a puzzling occurrence is fodder for the psychological mind. I couldn't stop thinking about it, and as I did, I began to see that what I had done so dramatically in my office, I had done to myself many times before. Perhaps with less flair, but nonetheless with equal effectiveness, I have allowed my self-doubt and fear of failure to sabotage my interests and cause me undue pain. And this process is not unique to me. Many of my friends and patients needlessly undermine their happiness through similar unconscious actions.

This book grew out of the events of that day. It is my attempt, not only to explain the phenomena of self-inflicted suffering, but to reveal how to stop it and live a more successful and fulfilling life. To be sure, popular psychology has investigated some aspects of the problem—such as procrastination, poor relationship choices, and fear of success—but it has never seen these issues as symptoms of a larger syndrome of behavior, what I call "Everyday Masochism" (EM). This is not the sexual masochism of whips and chains but of everyday punitive, undermining, and negating acts against the self.

I began my research with the assumption that this kind of self-abuse was more common than experts recognized, and I soon discovered my suspicions were right. Nearly half of the subjects I tested showed indications of thwarted assertion, low self-esteem, or guilt—all signs of EM. I also found, contrary to a widely held notion in psychology, that there are really four types of masochists: pleasers, martyrs, perfectionists, and avoiders—each distinguished by a particular history, style of action, and thought.

Yet Everyday Masochism is not simply an intrapersonal problem. The EM is a "natural" victim who falls prey to the victimizer. The two are drawn together in an irresistible relationship of dominance and submission that has the dark flavor of sadomasochism without the physical violence. Many of the troubles that plague intimate relationships in the eighties can be traced back to this dance. Lyricist Tom Lehrer has called it the "masochism tango," and, indeed, with its mindless repetition of steps and defined power roles of leader and follower, it has all the qualities of a dance. In this book I identify many of the more common tangos in work and personal relationships to show you how to recognize and deal with the six types of sadistic partners before they step on your toes. You may be surprised to find that these idividuals, obsessed by power and control, often feel as inadequate as their compliant counterparts.

What is the prognosis for the individual who appears drawn to gratuitous suffering and submission? Are Everyday Masochists forever damned to a life of frustration, anxiety, and depression? Certainly the path out is not as simple as weekend gurus would have us believe. Patterns of self-inflicted pain are deeply ingrained. A look at the psychological history of the EM gives ample evidence of that. Courage, patience, and commitment are needed to challenge the sense of guilt and unworth that underlie self-abusive patterns. But so tenacious is the grip of masochism that many who read this book will use its insights not to uplift but to further chastise and punish their already flagellated egos.

Still, there is reason to be hopeful. If we can understand the causes and origins of Everyday Masochism and become familiar with how it works in our lives, we can begin to change our behavior and, in turn, our feelings about ourselves. I outline the general rules for this retreat from pain throughout the book, and offer a program of daily exercises and techniques that have been designed to deal with the underlying causes of the problem. These tools have been highly effective in helping my patients learn how to get out of their own way and love and accept themselves. They can work for you, too.

Ultimately, Everyday Masochism is a condition rooted in low self-esteem and guilt. We judge too harshly and punish ourselves for exaggerated or imagined crimes. In this we are our own worst enemy, far more punitive than a jury of our peers. Perhaps we should remember an old legal maxim that has never seemed more relevant: *In propria causa nemo judex sit*—No one should be a judge in his own case! Taking such wisdom to heart is the first step toward freedom from self-abuse.

David Brandt, Ph.D.
Muir Beach, California

Chapter **One**

Beyond Whips and Chains

O, what a rogue and peasant slave am I!
SHAKESPEARE, *Hamlet*, Act II, Scene II

When the beauty shop called with a 4:30 cancellation, Janet jumped at the chance. She had finally taken a day off from her job as a paralegal and a new perm was just what she needed to lift her spirits. Lately she'd been feeling nearly invisible around her husband, and she hoped the change might attract his attention. While at the shop she decided to splurge and get her nails done, too. When she emerged into the late summer afternoon, she felt like a new woman—for about five minutes.

Checking her hair in the car's rearview mirror, Janet saw instead her nose, which she had never liked. Even in a full-length mirror, she always saw her nose first. Then she noticed a chin that was too prominent and eyes that were too small for her face. After that, she didn't want to look anymore. Though friends considered her attractive, bright, and capable, and told her so, she knew better. She was an overweight, overworked, thirty-five-year-old woman who wasn't much to look at and wasn't getting any younger. Her world revolved around her boss and husband, both of whom took her for granted. She looked in the mirror again. "So I've got new hair and nails," she thought. "Big deal. It's still the same old Janet."

She was nearly home when she suddenly realized that she'd forgotten to take the steaks out of the freezer. "Oh, no," she said aloud, "Richard'll hit the roof." She turned the car around and headed for the grocery store, feeling incapable of keeping even the kitchen together.

Janet was putting the groceries away when her husband came home from work. With a hollered hello, he went straight to his favorite chair, turned on the TV, and waited for Janet to bring him his drink.

"Thanks," he said. "Is dinner ready? I'm starved."

"I'm about to start it now," she said. "I just got home myself."

"What the hell have you been doing? I've been busting my ass at work while you've had the whole day to yourself. The least you can do is have dinner ready when I get home."

There didn't seem to be any point in mentioning the hairdresser. Richard hadn't seemed to notice her new perm, or if he had, he apparently didn't think it worth comment. "I'm sorry," she said. "I guess I just lost track of the time."

"What are you, too dumb to read your own watch? Do you need another clock around here?"

"I'm sorry," she repeated. "Do you want me to heat up last night's meatloaf?"

"I don't want leftovers," he snapped. "I want a steak. Do I have to make it myself?"

"Of course not," sighed Janet, "I'll start it right up."

"And get me another drink while you're at it."

"Coming right up." When Janet reached the kitchen, there were tears in her eyes. As she wiped them away she thought, "He's right. It's nobody's fault but my own."

*   *   *

Perhaps you know someone like Janet, or maybe you see some of yourself in her. Many of us unconsciously inflict psychic suffering on ourselves by harping on our own failings, exaggerating our inadequacies, doubting our abilities, and chronically submitting to the will of others. Such pain cannot be measured in physical scars or bruises. Its damage cannot be compensated by a court of law. Yet it is real, and the long-range emotional effects it produces are sometimes more destructive than tangible wounds.

Do You Fit the Following Description?
1. You'd rather accommodate to a difficult situation than stand up for yourself and risk a scene.
2. You always give the opinions, attitudes, and preferences of others more weight than you give your own.
3. You are your own worst critic; what you do never seems good enough.
4. You're always apologizing for yourself.
5. You're in a relationship that hurts you, but you hang on despite your own misgivings.
6. You feel compelled to explain and justify your behavior more than you'd like.
7. You feel underappreciated or abused at work.
8. You are afraid to stand up for yourself with your spouse or boss.

If more than two of these descriptions fit you, this is probably not the first time you've wondered why you are so self-destructive. Why you keep making the same mistakes. Why your heart always tells you to do one thing and your head another. And you're probably no closer to the answers than you were when you first posed these questions to yourself. Midnight talks with friends haven't provided a solution; neither have a myriad of self-help articles. In fact, no one seems to clearly understand your problem.

You're not crazy. You're not intellectually deficient. So

what's wrong? Why don't you learn from your mistakes? Why can't you shake these self-destructive patterns and live a happier and more successful life?

Sadly, you're not alone. A great many people live lives they feel are theirs by default rather than choice. Daily, they sabotage their own desires and long-term interests, while feeling powerless to change. Though the problem is not new, it has never been clearly addressed. Psychologists themselves are confused about the cause and etiology of this syndrome of behavior characterized by the irrational pursuit of unpleasure.

This book is written for you and for those who want to understand you. It is a map to the territory, a guidebook that identifies trouble spots, traps, and tough terrain. It will show you how things reached this point as well as the quickest and safest routes of escape.

THE PARADOX OF UNPLEASURE

Noted psychoanalyst Theodore Reik tells the story of a skier in Switzerland who, after encountering buffeting winds, freezing temperatures, and malfunctioning equipment, was inspired to write, "If you do not sprain your ankle, you break your leg, and if you do chance to keep your limbs whole, you still pass hours of humiliating and painful effort in very uncomfortable circumstances, when you might be spending your week's holiday at much less cost reading or sleeping by a warm fire, with a cat curled up on the mat. . . ." The would-be skier concluded with the satirical observation, "Man is a masochistic animal."

Although those tongue-in-cheek lines were written in 1936, they have an unmistakable current relevance. In fact, the view that we are largely masochistic animals straining under the yolk of an impersonal mass society run amok has never been more in fashion. Images of powerlessness, defeat at the hands of the system, and unnecessary personal suffering dot the contemporary landscape. From the hapless taxpayer intimidated by the threat of an IRS audit to the impotent credit card holder who struggles hopelessly to correct a computer error, there is a feeling that our destiny no longer lies in our own hands but in those of labyrinthian machines and anonymous men with their fingers on red buttons. In the broadest sense, any participation in this society sometimes feels like a masochistic act.

Yet philosophers (particularly the English) from Herbert Spencer to Bertrand Russell have asserted that we are primarily pleasure seekers or, at the very least, pain avoiders. Biologists note that even primitive, one-celled organisms move away from unpleasant stimulation toward more pleasurable environments. And common sense tells us that a choice between pleasure and pain is no choice at all. "Arsenic or scotch?" does not elicit serious debate.

But if these assumptions are true, how do we explain the pursuit of "unpleasure": the lure of the horror movie; the cultural preoccupation with blood and gore; the increasing fascination with sadomasochistic sex? If it is abundantly clear that all life is basically hedonistic, how do we interpret the actions of those who found themselves described in the statements posed a few pages earlier? Are they a breed apart, a species that defies natural law? Are they biologic mutants who commit acts of self-abuse against their will?

A patient of mine, whom I'll call Tom, is a perfectly healthy young man of thirty-two, gainfully employed, and moving steadily up the career ladder. But after an annual evaluation at work, Tom reported the following:

> When I got to the meeting with my supervisor, I was very nervous. Even though I knew she thought well of me, the very idea of being evaluated made me feel uncomfortable. It was clear after just a few minutes that she

was going to give me a glowing report and would recommend a substantial bonus. I was pleased, but I kept it to myself. Then when she hinted at the size of the bonus, something came over me. I actually heard myself request that she cut the amount in half. I justified the cut by pointing out some of my own failings, things I had wanted to keep private, especially from her. It was almost as if I couldn't help myself. I felt compelled to say it.

Fortunately for Tom, the supervisor knew good work when she saw it and was somewhat amused by what she assumed was staged humility. But Tom was not posturing; he was acting out of a sense of unworthiness. He had trouble accepting the bonus because some part of him felt that he didn't deserve it.

And this behavior was not atypical. At the most inopportune times, he sabotaged his hard-earned efforts. Once, after preparing for a special project for two weeks (fourteen or fifteen hours a day), he overslept and showed up late for the critical meeting. On another occasion he put off going to the doctor until a minor infection turned into a serious problem that nearly resulted in the amputation of a limb.

Surely Tom, who seems to pursue anything but pleasure, does not reflect the "man as hedonist" viewpoint. He constantly makes trouble for himself, provokes crises, and creates new suffering. Pleasure seems the furthest thing from his mind.

The Problem of Definition

The word *masochist* is generally used to describe those who are obliged to suffer, seem to enjoy their pain, and, if repetition indicates choice, prefer it to any other condition. It evokes images of long-handled whips, studded leather jackets, bound and helpless arms, and passionate shrieks of pain/

pleasure in the night. But masochism has come to mean more than sexual aberration. It is popularly used to describe any behavior that appears self-abusive, as in: "He's always in the library studying. What a masochist!"

Despite its new psychological chic, masochism is a word whose meaning is confused. There has been much historical and theoretical disagreement among the experts as to what it really is. And like so many clinical descriptions that have been usurped by the general public—depression and schizophrenia come to mind—it has become blandly generic.

The term was first used by the nineteenth-century sexologist Richard Krafft-Ebing to describe the individual who gets sexual satisfaction from the physical or psychological pain inflicted by another. It was inspired by Austrian novelist Leopold von Sacher-Masoch, whose books, particularly *Venus in Furs*, depicted men tortured and subjugated by domineering females.

Misunderstanding began when Sigmund Freud transported masochism from the strictly sexual sphere to the larger arena of social interaction. So much conflicting theory followed (including an about-face by the old master himself) that for years the term's meaning varied according to whom you talked to. Sadly, the situation has not changed much. There are arguments over whether masochism is exclusively sexual behavior or a way of relating to the world, over whether one actually must enjoy suffering or simply tolerate it, over whether patterns of chronic self-defeat alone qualify as true masochism, and over whether masochism is built into the female of the species as Freud had suggested.

EVERYDAY MASOCHISM

Because of this confusion and the macabre associations the term sometimes provokes, I use the phrase Everyday Masochism, EM, to describe the milder, ever-present self-abuse in daily life. Acts of sabotage (often unconscious), self-criticism and punishment, and repeated subordination of one's interests and needs are expressions of Everyday Masochism. In fact, any chronic pattern of self-negation has its roots in EM.

Everyday Masochism comes in two varieties: active and passive. Active forms include such behaviors as comparing oneself unfavorably to others, berating oneself for minor failings and mistakes, alarming oneself with catastrophic expectations, and seeking out incendiary information (perhaps the details of a spouse's affair). Passive forms—often more difficult to identify—include staying in a relationship with an abusive partner, remaining on a demeaning job, and colluding with a parent who refuses to treat you as an adult. (See A Dictionary of Masochism, Chapter 4, for additional examples.)

These behaviors are often not understood as masochism because they do not result in physical pain and are tolerated (rather than enjoyed) out of a sense of powerlessness and inadequacy. They may be lightweight when compared to the tortures engaged in by Dostoyevski's Raskolnikoff or a medieval flagellant, but to the extent that they represent self-inflicted, gratuitous suffering, they are a form of masochism that invariably takes a toll on self-esteem and performance.

All of us, save the most hardened psychopath, have a bit of EM in our psychological profiles. Yet it would be a mistake to jump to the conclusion that we are all Everyday Masochists. Showing some self-punitive behavior doesn't mean that all our motives are masochistic. Besides, certain actions can mislead the observer. Consider those hordes of grimacing joggers who pound the pavement every day. Are they indulging in "unpleasure" or ensuring their longevity through aerobic training? Acts that delay gratification for a greater reward down the road often appear self-abusive, but actually may be in the person's long-term interests. To avoid misclassification, we must know the context in which an action occurs and whether any unconscious motives are operating.

Individuals with high doses of Everyday Masochism represent a character style. They *behave* in a chronically acquiescent, passive, and self-punitive manner. Their underlying *attitude* toward themselves is marked by self-doubt and a sense of insufficiency. They tend to *perceive* or *interpret* events to support their view that life is beyond their control and that they are powerless to effect change.

EMs are always getting themselves caught in unequal relationships in which they are "one down." They repeatedly choose partners who are more interested in exercising power than expressing love and who try to dominate and control them. These partners are not necessarily bloodthirsty or evil; they are simply people who get satisfaction from putting down others and asserting their superiority. They are drawn to the Everyday Masochist like a predator to prey. The result is a curious and painful dance I call a "sadomasochistic tango." One dancer's interest in dominating perfectly complements the other's tendency to submit.

Yet though they may allow themselves to be walked over, this does not mean EMs are without virtue. On the contrary, they may be some of the most pleasing and charming individuals we know. They can be highly supportive, loyal, intensely interested in our problems, caring, and generous. But within themselves they feel inadequate and doubtful of their abilities, and they are rarely in contact with their own needs and wants.

Consider again my patient Tom. He is genuinely liked at work. Always friendly and anxious to please, he seems to have a special feeling for the underdog. His friends praise his self-sacrificing nature and point to the many unpaid hours he gives to the company youth program each year. Tom hasn't an enemy in the office and is considered loyal and trustworthy.

Still, you'd never know it to talk to him. After seven years in the same place, he is still uncertain how people feel about him. And when he cannot ignore the positive feelings of others toward him, he does his best to negate them. This is typical of EMs. Below the empathy and altruism lie restless individuals often confused and frustrated by their own sabotage. They desperately want approbation yet feel uncomfortable receiving it. The tension caused by this bind is responsible for much of their unhappiness.

Your Masochism Quotient

What is your Everyday Masochism quotient? Are you an incorrigible masochist or just an occasional sufferer? In the course of my research, I have constructed several tests to measure EM attitudes, feelings, and behaviors. To find out where you stand, take the test below. It will give you some indication of how serious a problem Everyday Masochism is for you.

Be honest with yourself and your score will more accurately reflect your EM level. Answer the questions according to the following: 1 = strong disagreement, 7 = strong agreement.

(circle one)

1. I am easily influenced by other people's opinions.   1 2 3 4 5 6 7
2. Getting angry only makes the situation worse.   1 2 3 4 5 6 7
3. At times, I feel I don't deserve to be happy.   1 2 3 4 5 6 7
4. I am a confident and self-assured person.   1 2 3 4 5 6 7
5. When things get really good, I don't expect them to last.   1 2 3 4 5 6 7

(circle one)

6. I often dwell on upsetting incidents
   from the past.   1 2 3 4 5 6 7
7. In competitive situations, I rarely
   doubt myself.   1 2 3 4 5 6 7
8. When I'm under pressure, I become
   critical of myself.   1 2 3 4 5 6 7
9. I have no trouble asserting for my
   needs and wants.   1 2 3 4 5 6 7
10. Criticism can be devastating to me.   1 2 3 4 5 6 7
11. I usually swallow my grievances rather
    than start an argument.   1 2 3 4 5 6 7
12. I usually play up my achievements and
    successes.   1 2 3 4 5 6 7
13. In new situations, I often feel like a
    fake.   1 2 3 4 5 6 7
14. When I compare myself to other people,
    I always come out ahead.   1 2 3 4 5 6 7
15. When I make a mistake, I'm usually
    hard on myself.   1 2 3 4 5 6 7
16. I take things more personally than
    other people seem to.   1 2 3 4 5 6 7
17. I wish someone would solve all my
    problems for me.   1 2 3 4 5 6 7
18. I often challenge people who have au-
    thority over me.   1 2 3 4 5 6 7
19. I often stay in disagreeable situations
    after I should have gotten out.   1 2 3 4 5 6 7
20. When someone disagrees with me, I'm
    likely to question myself.   1 2 3 4 5 6 7
21. I like to take risks, especially when the
    stakes are high.   1 2 3 4 5 6 7
22. It's easier to see faults in myself than
    in others.   1 2 3 4 5 6 7
23. I don't feel I'm as good as I should be.   1 2 3 4 5 6 7
24. When I face an important challenge, I
    usually think about all the things that
    might go wrong.   1 2 3 4 5 6 7

(circle one)

25. I don't believe in myself as much as
    I'd like to.   1 2 3 4 5 6 7
26. I sometimes put myself down in front
    of others.   1 2 3 4 5 6 7
27. I'm more likely to use caution than
    take a risk.   1 2 3 4 5 6 7
28. It's easy for me to tell someone that
    I'm angry at them.   1 2 3 4 5 6 7
29. I tend to focus on my shortcomings
    and limitations.   1 2 3 4 5 6 7
30. I usually act fast and decisively.   1 2 3 4 5 6 7
31. I feel guilty after I've indulged my-
    self.   1 2 3 4 5 6 7
32. I feel uncomfortable around people in
    authority.   1 2 3 4 5 6 7
33. It often seems difficult to live asser-
    tively in the world.   1 2 3 4 5 6 7
34. I rarely second-guess important deci-
    sions that I've made.   1 2 3 4 5 6 7
35. I feel uncomfortable receiving compli-
    ments.   1 2 3 4 5 6 7
36. Other people's anger disturbs me.   1 2 3 4 5 6 7
37. I am a good advocate for myself.   1 2 3 4 5 6 7
38. If something goes wrong, I usually
    blame myself.   1 2 3 4 5 6 7
39. I find it easy to accept criticism.   1 2 3 4 5 6 7
40. It's hard for me to enjoy myself if
    there's work to be done.   1 2 3 4 5 6 7
41. I sometimes feel I'm not a worthwhile
    person.   1 2 3 4 5 6 7
42. I'm afraid I might lose control if I get
    angry.   1 2 3 4 5 6 7
43. It is easier to stand up for others than
    for myself.   1 2 3 4 5 6 7
44. I feel guilty when I say "no."   1 2 3 4 5 6 7
45. I'm afraid that if people really knew
    me, they would be disappointed.   1 2 3 4 5 6 7

Give the test to your spouse or lover and compare results. What can you learn from them? Which one of you is more likely to be passive in conflict situations? Controlling? Submissive? Now take the test for your partner; answer the questions as you think they describe him or her and compare the numbers you come up with against your partner's actual score. Is there a discrepancy? One married couple who did this got curious results. Each identified the other as more masochistic than the partner rated himself. In discussing the differences, both agreed that their spouse's perception was probably more accurate than their own, which was somewhat idealized.

46. I have complete confidence in my
    skills and abilities.   1 2 3

47. It's easier to see what's wrong about
    myself than what's right.   1 2 3

48. Frequently, I am aware of angry feel-
    ings only after the situation has
    passed.   1 2 3 4

49. I know what I want and how to get it.   1 2 3 4

50. I give other people's opinions more
    weight than my own.   1 2 3 4

Scoring the Test

STEP 1. Total your scores on the following questions: 4, 7, 9
         14, 18, 22, 28, 30, 34, 37, 39, 46, and 49.

STEP 2. Total your scores on all the other items.

STEP 3. Subtract the first total from the second to determine
         your raw score.

STEP 4. Check your raw score against the following table.
         Below 90 =   No evidence of Everyday Masochism
         90 to 105 =   Slight tendency
         106 to 125 = Moderate tendency
         126 to 139 = Strong tendency
         140+   = Very high EM level

Other Ways to Use the Scale

Once you have calculated your raw score, go back to the test
questions for a qualitative check. Note which items received a
6 or more. What do these items measure? For example, if you
had high scores on questions 2, 11, 28, 36, and 42, you have a
problem expressing anger. An item-by-item analysis will give
you an indication of the specific areas in which your masochism exists.

Chapter **Two**

Not for the Love of Suffering

I can never be satisfied with anyone who
would be blockhead enough to have me.

ABRAHAM LINCOLN

Now that you have an indication of your EM quotient, you
may be saying to yourself, "Even though I do some of these
things, I don't really want to suffer. I'd rather be happy than
miserable. Therefore, I can't really be a masochist." This is a
good point, one that leads us to an important fact about the
"pursuit of unpleasure." Although it is commonly held that
Everyday Masochists want to suffer and enjoy pain, nothing
is further from the truth. Reik was first to note that these
people do not get gratification from pain. Suffering is accepted as a means to an end, not as an end in itself. Masochists tolerate suffering as the price they must pay to earn the
right to satisfaction. It is suffering that provides the moral
capital used to buy one's needs and preferences. If I am overworked, overstressed, and overwhelmed, I can justify a vaca-

35

tion in paradise. If I am maligned, abused, and manipulated, I have earned the right to be angry.

Often, these individuals feel they deserve to suffer, for masochistic souls are laden with a deep sense of culpability. They feel responsible for past crimes, real and imagined. An all-pervasive sense of guilt plays a role in most decisions and actions. Unconsciously, they seek punishment in order to cleanse themselves of guilt feelings.

Self-punishers also tolerate suffering because they feel powerless: They do not believe they can change the way they live their lives. They view events as happening to them; they are acted upon instead of acting on. They don't feel that they have the discipline, vigilance, or energy required to behave in any other manner. And they don't believe they have control or real influence over what they feel.

Even if they possessed the personal power to make an impact on circumstances, these people would not know how to reshape them for the better. Everyday Masochists may be insightful about many things, but not about alternatives to their self-defeating actions and attitudes. Afraid to assert themselves, they see direct interpersonal confrontations as disastrous and certain to fail. In order to survive such situations, they try to neutralize aggression by submitting or by attacking themselves. They show their vulnerability, hoping that their "enemies" will respond charitably to this show of weakness.

On first impression, this seems like a rather ineffective way to survive. But think about it. Have you ever been self-critical to keep someone else from pointing out your failings? Have you ever apologized for something that you knew was not your fault, or broken down in tears in order to manipulate your lover?

Being submissive to get what you want may seem paradoxical, but sometimes it can be an effective strategy. In Reik's view, masochists exercise indirect control of events by revealing their weaknesses and being willing to tolerate anything the sadist dishes out. They win by outlasting their opponent's cruelty.

Examples of this strategy can be found in the animal kingdom where the capacity for masochistic behavior appears to have species survival value. The timber wolf will place itself in a submissive position by exposing its jugular vein after it has lost a battle to another wolf. On seeing this sign, the victor will spare the life of its antagonist. A similar mechanism exists in the turkey cock, thereby ensuring that the species will be protected from the unrestrained aggression of its own kind.

Wilhelm Reich, the brilliant psychiatrist who took on the Freudian establishment, added another twist to this perspective. Reich believed (and here I am taking liberties by broadening his concept) that masochists castigate themselves in order to deflect attention from what they really fear. For example, if they are afraid of being revealed as stupid or incompetent, they may publicly criticize themselves for something like procrastinating or always arriving late. They select a second-rate issue on which to deprecate themselves in order to direct attention away from the really humiliating flaw that haunts them.

Reich's hypothesis is supported by studies on pain management, which indicate that predictable pain is overwhelmingly preferred to unpredictable pain. When the subject knows it is coming or when he or she controls its beginning and end, the pain is much easier to tolerate. Could this be why EMs put themselves down in public? Since they believe they will be exposed anyway, they can at least control the focus of that exposure.

I once asked a member of one of my therapy groups why she was so critical of herself in front of the others. Her frankness surprised me. "People feel sorry for me when I point out certain faults," she said. "They tell me I'm too self-critical, that I'm really no different than anyone else and should be nicer to myself. I can keep them away from my darker feelings this way. They accept these unimportant problems as the real thing. If they only knew what I really fell about myself. . . ."

A final thought on the "why" of suffering: At the root of all masochists' feelings about themselves is a deep sense of disappointment. They do not measure up to their own expectations. And no matter how positive or affirming their experiences, that hard-core sense of insufficiency refuses to die. This is not because they are truly valueless, but because they have constructed an idealized vision of what they should be that is inconsistent with who they really are.

This constant comparison with the perfect "self" leads to an ever-present feeling of worthlessness that shapes their experience. Always disappointed, they have a tough time believing in themselves or anything associated with them.

A TRIAD OF TRAITS

The motives of Everyday Masochists are complex and cannot be reduced to the love of suffering, yet at the core of every EM are three personality characteristics—what I call the masochistic triad—from which all self-inflicted pain originates. They are (1) power failure, (2) low self-esteem, and (3) unconscious guilt. Though fundamental to the Everyday Masochist, they are often hidden from view. They may not appear obvious to friends and colleagues, but make no mistake, they exist under the thin veneer of confidence and control. EMs are all too familiar with the triad although they may not associate it with masochism.

Power Failure

Everyday Masochists don't recognize their power, their ability to influence events. They don't use their natural authority to meet their needs. In fact, they are afraid of their own healthy aggression. They think it will overwhelm them and alienate those around them so, instead, they allow others to control their destiny, accommodating rather than risking assertion.

MISDIRECTED ANGER: Nowhere is this better illustrated than in the individual's relationship to anger. EMs find it difficult to express this emotion directly. They see only the imagined negative consequences of stating their feelings: "My lover will leave if I stand up to her"; "My friends will ridicule me if I tell them how I really feel"; "My boss will let me have it if I express my anger."

There is always a convenient rationalization about why it is better to keep resentments hidden. But in fact, these people are frightened of their own aggression. They are unfamiliar with it, and its possible consequences—rejection, disapproval, loss of control—terrify them.

This is not to say that EMs don't feel anger. But only occasionally do they *express* it, and then only to those in an obviously weaker position. Children, older people, and subordinates are common targets. With equals or superiors, they take an indirect tack, expressing their resentment passively, hiding behind obstinacy, deliberate forgetting, sarcasm, and contrariness. These safe actions disguise their real motives, allowing them to eliminate the risk of being held accountable.

Everyday Masochists distance themselves from their aggressive feelings by focusing on emotions that are more familiar and less dangerous (though not necessarily more pleasant).

Feelings of sadness, hurt, or even confusion frequently mask deeper animosities. It is far more tolerable for EMs to acknowledge being wronged or victimized than admit to feeling outraged, and most of the time this emotional substitution occurs without conscious awareness.

A more common way of mitigating their aggressive feelings is to turn them back on themselves. Indeed, a great deal of the Everyday Masochist's faultfinding, condemnation, and self-reproach is the result of this sort of "retroflexion." In stead of feeling resentful of a critical boss who is never satisfied, they will view their own performance as deficient and kick themselves for not doing a better job. It is certainly easier to assume blame than risk the consequences of faulting someone else.

THWARTED SELF-ASSERTION: Along with problems in expressing anger, EMs have trouble asserting themselves. When sitting behind "talkers" at the movies, they find it difficult to ask them to quiet down. Though annoyed, they won't confront a person who breaks in front of them on line. They have difficulty bringing a faulty item back to the store. They buy things they don't need because they can't say "no" to the salesperson.

Assertion plainly embarrasses them. EMs feel they don't have the right to stand up for themselves. They also fear they will be challenged. In the midst of an interaction, they undermine their assertion by "identifying" with the other person's position—the other's rightness—often losing touch with their own claims. A patient of mine asked her supervisor for a raise by saying, "I know you're having a tough time staying within your department's budget, but if there's any way that you could give me a pay increase. . . ." Her phrasing sabotaged the request by emphasizing the boss's perspective (tight budget) rather than hers (I need more and I'm worth it). It also provided the boss with a ready-made excuse for refusing.

Everyday Masochists feel so vulnerable when standing up for themselves that they only half try. Asserting for others is an altogether different matter, however. The very fact that they are asking for someone else gives them a sense of greater legitimacy.

THE GUILTY "NO": The issue of thwarted assertion shows up most dramatically in their difficulty with setting limits. EMs have trouble saying "no," whether it be to a boss, lover, or best friend. Thus, they may take on a work assignment that they have no time for, offer to do an errand that severely inconveniences them, or fail to hold consistently to family rules they have themselves established.

Saying "no" makes them feel guilty. They believe that good employees should always do what is requested of them. True friends must always come through. Not meeting these idealized standards puts them in the wrong. They fear they will be attacked or fired for setting limits. Hence, they often appear to be nice guys, team players who accommodate for the greater good, when in reality resentment may be smoldering below the surface.

OBSTRUCTED WILL: The power failure of the Everyday Masochist can be traced back to an obstructed will. Will is the assertion of one's self on the world, the capacity to fulfill goals and make real choices. EMs often feel uncertain and hesitant, as if they're not quite up to the task at hand. They view life's challenges as overwhelming and impossible instead of as opportunities for personal betterment. Acutely aware of past failures, they frequently remind themselves of their limitations just when they need to be energized with visions of what they can be.

Passivity is the natural outcome of a thwarted will. Everyday Masochists believe that the locus of control is outside themselves, that things happen to them, and that they must make the best of their situation. "Why even try" is the predictable response of someone who sees no means of changing things.

LEARNING TO BE HELPLESS: If I place a dog in a laboratory situation, I can teach him rather easily to avoid getting shocked by pushing a lever in front of him. But if I then place the same dog in a similar situation and make it impossible for him to escape the shock, unexpected things begin to happen. If I now try to teach him to press the lever and avoid punishment, he will fail to learn what came so easily before. He may whimper, moan, and try to escape, but he will not relearn to push the lever that stops the pain. In effect, he has been trained to act helplessly. He has been taught by experience that he has no control over events, so that even when the possiblity of control is reinstated, he doesn't act.

This is the EMs story, too. They have been conditioned by early life events to believe that they have very limited impact over the circumstances of their lives. They have learned to feel and act helplessly. And like the dog in the laboratory, when there are opportunities to take control, they will not recognize or accept them. The consequence is a sense of personal inertia that is itself deeply troubling.

Another expression of basic passivity is the failure of EMs to initiate. In social interactions, this takes the form of waiting for the other person to choose the topic or direction of conversation or even to determine when the discussion is over. Everyday Masochists don't recognize the degree of influence they can bring to bear simply by asking a question or changing the topic. When they do ask a question, it is often hiding an opinion that they are hesitant to express directly. Thus, they may ask their escort, "Do you want to stay at this party?" when what they really feel is "I'm not having a good time and I want to leave."

All this should not be taken to mean that every EM feels as helpless as dust in the wind. Though many have difficulty expressing anger, asserting themselves, initiating, and setting limits, they often manipulate the environment in indirect ways. They may not feel capable of creating events, but they are experienced at sabotaging them. For example, they may undermine a meeting they don't want to attend by arriving late. Or they may behave coolly toward a lover in order to get him or her to end the relationship.

Low Self-Esteem

Everyday Masochists have an inordinately negative view of themselves. They feel deficient, that something is wrong with them, and that their value is questionable. In the language of popular psychology, they are not "okay."

During a therapy session, I asked a patient to close her eyes and imagine herself in a lovely garden with a wishing well and many varieties of flowers. After only a few moments, she told me that the garden was beautiful but she couldn't really see it. She had visualized herself at the bottom of the well, lying on her back, small, helpless, and unable to get out. The obvious interpretation that she viewed herself as insignificant and invisible alarmed her, but she agreed that it was correct. Indeed, she had frequently admitted to feeling valueless, easily overlooked, and powerless to change. Her imagination provided an accurate picture of just how she saw herself.

Another patient, who had recently married, confessed, "I'm afraid I don't have enough for him. I'll let him down; I'll fail him. What I have to offer is too little, and he'll resent me for it and end up leaving because I couldn't give him the sympathy, understanding, and tenderness he needs."

What these two women have in common is a poor sense of their full value as people. Although both have achieved a measure of worldly success, they continue to view themselves as flawed and undesirable. Consequently, they underestimate their intelligence, physical attractiveness, and general competence, typically exaggerating their inadequacies and flaws. Their low opinion of themselves taints everything associated with them. Their jobs are not really important, their homes are second-rate, even their clothes are drab and unexciting.

DOUBTING THE SELF: An inevitable by-product of low self-esteem is self-doubt. How can I value my own opinion if I don't value myself? Everyday Masochists seek advice more than is necessary because they don't trust their own intuition, instincts, physical sensations, and powers of deduction. This search for answers from friends and experts ironically reinforces their sense of inadequacy and failed confidence.

Self-doubt shows itself most clearly in the equivocating language of EMs. It is seen in disqualifying statements: "I may be wrong about this, but . . ."; in the overuse of apology: the favorite phrase being "I'm sorry"; and in elaborate and unnecessary justifications: "I can't come because it's my son's birthday *and* the dog is sick *and* I have a cold."

ADDICTION TO APPROVAL: The negative self-image EMs hold is further reflected in their intense need to win the approval of others. If narcissists are in love with themselves, masochists are enamored with the love of others. In some ways they are addicted to it. They care too much about how others see them; whether the comment they have just made will be taken with offense; whether their canceling a date with a friend will result in their being disliked or discarded. This is why they usually assume the "nice person" role. Indeed, they meet the idea of being a little less sweet or compliant with strong opposition, typically rationalizing it away with the comment, "I see nothing wrong with caring about others; the world would be a better place if everyone were nicer to each other." True enough, but they are literally afraid of being anything but nice. Their altruism is motivated less by their desire for a more benevolent world than by their desperation to be loved.

EMs use the approval of others for a quick fix of "okay-ness." If others see them as worthwhile, then indeed it must be so. But approval provides only a momentary rise in self-esteem and never really penetrates the feelings of inadequacy. These remain untouched and continue to feed their sense of insufficiency.

As hooked as they are to approval, Everyday Masochists are equally concerned with avoiding its opposite. Criticism is devastating to them. They experience it as humiliating; the deep secret of their deficiency has been revealed. Even a quick disapproving glance, a fleeting look of disappointment or impatience from a person they want to please, can be blown out of proportion to mean they have been dressed down. Evading disapproval is probably a stronger motive than gaining the love of others.

Unconscious Guilt

Guilt, the most common and fundamental feeling that Everyday Masochists experience, is the driving force behind self-inflicted suffering. Every aspect of their lives is pervaded by it. It cuts across all experience and is a relative constant in dreams and fantasies. EMs often feel ashamed of their thoughts and actions. And no matter how benevolent or generous they seem, they cannot shake this view of themselves as wrong and blameworthy.

Guilt is strictly a human phenomenon. There is no such emotion in the animal kingdom. Unlike some feelings, which are immediate reactions to the perception of objects or events, guilt, like sentimentality, is built on an idea. We feel guilty when we *think* we have violated a social or moral standard: "I should have been a better friend" or "I shouldn't have lost my temper." EMs are dominated by "shoulds" and therefore habitually suffer from guilt pangs.

Excessive guilt leads to the development of what some therapists call an overactive "inner critic"—that part of us that is always harping on mistakes and inadequacies. The inner critic sits on our shoulders like the strictest grammar school teacher whispering such things as: "You really didn't do enough"; "You should have known better"; "You didn't stand up for yourself." Its contemptuous drone is so constant that most masochists experience it as background music and are unaware of how pervasive the message really is.

When plans do not work out, someone is unhappy, or there is a difference of opinion, the critic is particularly active, castigating and berating, driving home its punishing message. Even when the individual is an obvious victim of circumstance, the inner tormentor will distort enough facts to place the blame on him.

Self-denial is another way Everyday Masochists express their guilt. In a society gone crazy for every form of hedonism from drugs to hot tubs, their asceticism seems oddly out of step. EMs feel undeserving of pleasure and suspect that something bad will happen to them if they indulge themselves. For them, pleasure should be earned and is best kept contained within ritualized boundaries, such as Saturday nights or weekends. But even then it must be carefully watched. You can never tell when it will get addictive.

Everyday Masochists suffer from *"anhedonia,"* the psychological term for the inability to experience pleasure. For example, EMs feel uncomfortable taking vacations and may refuse them unless they're absolutely exhausted and therefore entitled to a respite. It then takes them most of the holiday to adjust to being free of responsibility. When they finally surrender to relaxation, they really begin to worry—"What if the return flight is late?" "What if the kids are sick?" "What if. . . ?"—until they have worked themselves back into a state of anxiety. Not until they see the end of the vacation at hand do they begin to loosen up. Now they can finally enjoy themselves (because it will be over soon) and return with glowing reports about what a wonderful time they had.

Compliments are another bugaboo. Everyone likes to get them, right? Not Everyday Masochists. They feel genuinely uncomfortable with the praise of friends. They are suspect of the compliment's sincerity because they cannot see the admired qualities in themselves. They also feel embarrassed by the attention. Underneath their embarrassment, however, they are really quite pleased; they simply have trouble receiving praise, often feeling they must discredit it or quickly pass onto something else. In effect, their discomfort diminishes not only their pleasure but also the opinion of the speaker who has offered the tribute.

In the slightly amended words of octogenarian philosopher George Burns, a masochist "Feels bad when he feels good for fear that he'll feel worse when he feels better."

Chapter **Three**

Profiles in Masochism

Thou has not half that power to do me
harm
As I have to be hurt

SHAKESPEARE, *Othello*, Act V, Scene II

> ARISTOTLE: This is wonderful writing. Brilliant, timeless stuff.
>
> PLATO: It's garbage and you know it.
>
>   *   *   *
>
> MARTHA: You're late. I've been waiting half an hour.
>
> GEORGE: Sorry, I had a really long day.
>
> MARTHA: Well, dinner's cold and I've got a headache.
>
> GEORGE: Martha, crossing the Delaware is no picnic. Look, I'll make it up to you. Why don't I take you out to your favorite restaurant instead?
>
> MARTHA: No, forget it. It's too late and I'm too tired. Besides, I've lost my appetite.

Plato and Martha demonstrate two kinds of masochistic behavior. One refuses himself the pleasure of praise, the other is intent on remaining miserable no matter what the circumstances. Their differences raise an interesting question. Is

48

there more than one type of social masochist? Though psychological theorists have always contended that there is only one kind, the incredible variation in self-abusive behavior suggests otherwise. Everyday Masochists are not all alike. Some are complainers, others are stoics. Some nurse their suffering, while others try to hide from it. Though all are linked by the triad of traits suggested in Chapter 2, they express themselves differently in the world.

My research indicates that there are really four EM types—perfectionist, pleaser, martyr, and avoider—and though there is usually overlap among categories (there are very few pure types), it helps to see them as distinct entities.

THE TYPE TEST

If your score on the EM scale suggests some masochism, take the test below to find out what type you are. Remember, you may uncover more than one tendency within yourself. Respond to the questions according to the following:

1 = strong disagreement; 7 = strong agreement

1. I am not happy unless I do the best
   job possible.   1 2 3 4 5 6 7
2. I don't get the appreciation I deserve.   1 2 3 4 5 6 7
3. Being liked is more important than
   anything else.   1 2 3 4 5 6 7
4. I tend to put things off until the last
   minute.   1 2 3 4 5 6 7
5. Failing at something is one of the
   worst experiences in life.   1 2 3 4 5 6 7
6. I often feel I haven't gotten a fair
   shake in life.   1 2 3 4 5 6 7
7. I try to live up to other people's expec-
   tations.   1 2 3 4 5 6 7
8. I usually let difficult situations resolve
   themselves.   1 2 3 4 5 6 7

9. If I don't set the highest standards for
myself, I won't do well.   1 2 3 4 5 6 7

10. I often feel misjudged and treated
wrongly.   1 2 3 4 5 6 7

11. I often apologize for my behavior and
opinions.   1 2 3 4 5 6 7

12. When a problem occurs, I'd just as
soon let someone else deal with it.   1 2 3 4 5 6 7

13. I'm hard on myself when I make the
same mistake twice.   1 2 3 4 5 6 7

14. I have more adversity in my life than
others do.   1 2 3 4 5 6 7

15. I feel guilty when I don't respond with
generosity.   1 2 3 4 5 6 7

16. Things usually work themselves out
without my taking action.   1 2 3 4 5 6 7

17. I feel as if I have to constantly prove
myself.   1 2 3 4 5 6 7

18. I never seem to get the breaks that
others do.   1 2 3 4 5 6 7

19. I usually tone down my opinions to
avoid an argument.   1 2 3 4 5 6 7

20. I sometimes spend a whole weekend
watching TV, sleeping, or binging on
food.   1 2 3 4 5 6 7

21. My real intentions are often misunder-
stood.   1 2 3 4 5 6 7

22. I worry about what kind of impression
I make on others.   1 2 3 4 5 6 7

23. I cannot accept average performance.   1 2 3 4 5 6 7

24. When I have an important decision to
make, I often want to escape.   1 2 3 4 5 6 7

25. I feel saddled with many insolvable
problems.   1 2 3 4 5 6 7

26. If I'm unfriendly or brusque, I worry
that others will resent me.   1 2 3 4 5 6 7

27. If I can't excel at something, I'm not
that interested in it.   1 2 3 4 5 6 7

28. I tend to keep my problems at a distance.   1 2 3 4 5 6 7
29. It's hard not to envy people who have what I want.   1 2 3 4 5 6 7
30. I'm very careful not to hurt other people's feelings.   1 2 3 4 5 6 7
31. When I make a mistake, getting angry at myself motivates me to do better.   1 2 3 4 5 6 7
32. I don't reflect much on my feelings.   1 2 3 4 5 6 7
33. I've been treated unfairly by many people in my life.   1 2 3 4 5 6 7
34. I'm not a boat rocker; I don't like to make waves.   1 2 3 4 5 6 7
35. I set very high standards for my own performance.   1 2 3 4 5 6 7
36. There are some things about myself I'd rather not know.   1 2 3 4 5 6 7
37. I have a hard time forgiving those who've wronged me.   1 2 3 4 5 6 7
38. I'm more often the giver than the receiver.   1 2 3 4 5 6 7
39. I usually feel I should do better than I've done.   1 2 3 4 5 6 7
40. I have a hard time handling emotional scenes.   1 2 3 4 5 6 7

Scoring the Test

STEP 1. Total your scores on items: 1, 5, 9, 13, 17, 23, 27, 31, 35, and 39.   Score A _____

Step 2. Total your scores on items: 3, 7, 11, 15, 19, 22, 26, 30, 34, and 38.   Score B _____

Step 3. Total your scores on items: 2, 6, 10, 14, 18, 21, 25, 29, 33, and 37.   Score C _____

Step 4. Total your scores on items: 4, 8, 12, 16, 20, 24, 28, 32, 36, and 40.   Score D _____

Score A measures perfectionist type; B measures pleaser type; C measures martyr type; and D measures avoider type.

Step 5.   Use the table below to check your tendency toward a particular EM type:

> Below 40 = no tendency
> 40 to 44 = mild tendency
> 45 to 49 = moderate tendency
> 50 to 54 = strong tendency
> 55 + = very high profile

Now that you have some indication of your EM type(s), see the profiles below to find out what each one describes. You may also want to use this scale in other ways. Consult the test in Chapter 1 for suggestions.

PROFILE 1: THE PERFECTIONIST

Recognizable Features:

Fits Goethe's description: "He is a man whom it is impossible to please because he is never pleased with himself."

Tries harder than necessary; must give 100 percent every time or feels worthless.

Pays excessive attention to detail.

Sets impossible goals and strains to meet them.

Cautious; plans all actions ahead of time.

Tends toward worry and depression.

Shows inflexibility, particularly toward change.

Fears spontaneity; afraid of losing control.

Attitudes and Beliefs:

Straining for perfection produces excellence, and saves one from mediocrity.

People who perform at normal levels are second-rate, and there is nothing worse than that.

Successful people achieve success with minimal effort and little error.

Satisfaction comes only from outstanding performance.

Repeating the same mistake twice shows a lack of character.

Childhood: Parents link love to high performance; only successful behavior is rewarded.

Message to child: "You will be loved only if you are successful."

Child feels worth and caring contingent on winning; must be successful at all costs.

Work: Tends to overwork; creates possibility of early burnout.

Less productive than would like; works past the point of diminishing returns.

Misses the big picture; may sabotage efforts with too much focus on detail.

Creativity stifled by unwillingness to make an error or take a risk.

Rulebound.

Fear of failure and underlying self-doubt result in overpreparation, worry, and occasional panic.

May be hypercritical as a supervisor, demanding too much from subordinates and creating resentment.

Uses fear to motivate self; imagines consequences of poor performance to galvanize self into action.

Intimate Relationships:	Not given to self-disclosure; afraid to reveal or admit vulnerabilities.
	Reacts defensively to criticism and suggestion.
	Believes his way is the right way.
	Sets inflexible expectations for partner and over-reacts to disappointment.
	Can tyrannize partner with same impossible standards applied to self.
	Sets rigid rules to govern relationship.
	Does not easily compromise; stubborn.
	Is afraid of being rejected for imperfections.
Sex:	Relies on sexual rituals; lovemaking must proceed in a particular way.
	Has trouble relaxing and letting down to sensuality.
	Sex is work, yet another area that demands performance.
	May be hypercritical of partner's lovemaking.
	Sees changes in lovemaking patterns as threatening.
	Cannot surrender to passion; always maintains self-control.
Male/ Female Ratio:	Males are more prone to this type of masochism because of sex-role emphasis on productivity and performance. With changing sex roles, women are showing up more and more in this category.
Analysis:	Perfectionists' greatest fear is being second-rate, which is tantamount to being worthless. Their

value as people is directly proportional to how well they perform. The goals they set are impossibly high, so they struggle compulsively but unsuccessfully to meet them. The absolute demand for perfection creates excessive worry, overattention to detail, loneliness, and depression. By pushing too hard, perfectionists lose sight of priorities and alienate those around them. Research shows that they are actually less successful than others who do not drive themselves with the same obsessive abandon.

Perfectionists are dominated by ironclad rules that govern all their thoughts and actions. Though all EM personalities are oppressed by such rules, perfectionists' "shoulds" tend to be more rigid and moralistic. Examples: "I should be able to endure hardships without complaint"; "I should never make an error"; "I should always operate at the highest level of efficiency."

Perfectionists' thinking is distorted in three ways: (1) They tend to see only the flaw in their performance, which they use to berate themselves. They overlook the positive. (2) They see the world in all-or-nothing terms so that if they are not entirely successful, they have failed. They don't acknowledge the middle ground between the two extremes. (3) They reach a general conclusion based on a single incident. If they fail a test, they extend this to mean that they are bad students, inadequate lovers, or second-rate racquetball players.

Perfectionists can never feel more than temporary satisfaction because they have given themselves an impossible and never-ending task. Their self-denigration is a response to their failure to meet an ideal that doesn't exist in reality.

Help: *Step 1:* Recognize that straining toward impossible goals does not produce the desired success but in fact stands in its way.

Step 2: Break the link between self-worth and performance. Acknowledge that no one is worthless because of imperfections.

Step 3: Accept yourself, warts and all.

EXAMPLE: Bruce is a professional tennis player who has been on the international tour for the past three years. At twenty-five, he is still young enough to improve his game and his ranking in the United States Tennis Association's standings. Since turning pro after college, he has had an inconsistent career plagued by long slumps. Though he has played brilliantly at times, showing great promise, he has also been mediocre.

Bruce's personal life is marked by the same intensity as his tennis game. He has moved through a succession of six-month relationships, always finding some critical fault in his partner before things get serious. Touring makes keeping up with friends difficult, but even if he had a more stable life, Bruce would not be surrounded by people. His style is one of isolation and introspection.

Like most perfectionists, Bruce is hung up on success—winning is everything. His striving is obvious in the number of hours he spends practicing his game. He is unforgiving of his errors and demands of himself absolute commitment to every point.

Bruce's drive to succeed is actually part of his problem. He cannot tolerate the thought that he might be a mediocre professional, just another player on the tour. Because his value as a person is contingent on his professional success, every match becomes a test of self-worth. The pressure created by such thinking is too great a burden to carry through the whole season and explains why he has not lived up to his potential.

As his coach says, "If Bruce would just get off his own back and not ride himself about every missed point and lost opportunity, his game would improve. His concentration is weakened by his inability to let go of past errors. He simply cannot tolerate making a mistake."

"Sometimes I just feel I'm going to lose," Bruce says. "I can't tell whether it's my fear speaking or whether it's prophecy, but when I feel that way before a tournament, I never play well."

Because he is so preoccupied with images of doom, Bruce can't focus on the internal cues that allow an athlete to perform at the highest level of capability. He tries to use fear as a motivator, feeding himself images of failure to galvanize him into action, but the strategy boomerangs. He creates so much nervous energy that he pushes his shots. By trying too hard, Bruce generates tension when he needs relaxed confidence.

Here we can see how the perfectionist, preoccupied with performance and the fear of failure, actually impedes success. Bruce believes that if he doesn't push himself, he'll be just another player. In fact, his striving, more than any other single factor, predisposes him to mediocrity.

The same rules apply off the court. In his relationships, Bruce imposes the same excessive standards on his partners. They are never quite good enough; there is always some major flaw that he cannot tolerate. He admonishes them to try harder, but eventually, if he doesn't lose interest, they do. No one wants to play Eliza Doolittle to his Henry Higgins.

PROFILE 2: THE PLEASER

Recognizable Features:	Concerned and sympathetic, especially for the underdog.
	Is a good friend, supportive, and attentive.
	Suffers from stewardess syndrome: always pleasant, affable, and congenial.
	Worries unduly about what others think of him or her.
	Is compliant; accommodates rather than asserts own needs.
	Apologizes frequently for self.
	Doesn't rock the boat; likes to blend in.
	Is obedient and easily intimidated by authority.
	Compulsively places self in the service of others.
Attitudes and Beliefs:	Being liked is the most important thing in life.
	Expressing one's own needs will drive others away.
	People who don't extend themselves to others won't be valued.
	Anger is destructive and should be suppressed; it's always better to turn the other cheek.
	Giving in to another's demands for the sake of peace is a virtue.
	If something goes wrong, it's probably my fault.
Childhood:	Parents equate approval and love; only pleasing behavior is rewarded.

Message to child: "You will be loved if you are good [meet our expectations]. When you are not good, you hurt us."

Child feels self-worth is contingent on how well he or she meets the expectations of others. Feels guilty for acts of self-assertion.

Work:

Is a loyal and generally hard-working employee; approval of supervisors is very important.

Rarely makes it to the top; too concerned with being liked, too self-effacing.

Can stand up for company but not for self; has trouble asking for raises, days off, and so on.

Has difficulty setting limits on boss's demands.

Is uncomfortable in authority roles; disciplining out-of-line subordinates is particularly hard.

Often feels overwhelmed by demands of job; doesn't delegate responsibility well.

High percentage found in helping professions.

Intimate Relationships:

Allows partner to assume power; takes inferior role.

Avoids conflict by blaming self for problems.

Gives more than receives.

When partner doesn't reciprocate generosity, usually tries to win him or her over with more giving.

Rescues partner even when help is not solicited.

Doesn't assert own needs; lets others run over him or her.

Is frequently more aware of partner's needs than his or her own; often puts other's preferences ahead of own.

Shows confessional behavior; feels compelled to be candid about own weaknesses and limitations.

Sex: Can be sensitive lover; aware of partner's feelings.

Gives pleasure easily but has trouble receiving it.

Worries about desirability, whether lover is really turned on to him or her.

Often takes subordinate position; waits instead of initiating.

May engage in submission and domination scenes; feels more comfortable in the inferior role.

May fake orgasm to please partner.

Male/
Female   Found in both sexes, but the percentage of females is higher.
Ratio:

Analysis: Pleasers are archetypical "good boys and girls," who, despite the fact that they follow the program 100 percent, are usually plagued by self-doubt. Though other EM types seek approval as a matter of course, pleasers take the process one step further: They ignore or override their own interests to win the goodwill of their peers or superiors because they equate love with approval. Uncertain of their value, being liked by others is the most important thing in their lives.

To win approbation, pleasers believe they must meet everyone's expectations for them. Their sincerity, acquiescence, and self-effacement are intended to win favor and ward off criticism. Consequently, how others see them is of critical importance. In their haste for the respect of friends and co-workers, they often overextend themselves. They feel that if they say "no," people will turn on them.

Rescuing others is one way pleasers try to win favor. By saving someone from difficulty, they are doing the "right thing" and at the same time ensuring themselves of continued goodwill. Pleasers give to get. They reach out to others with extraordinary generosity, often putting themselves last. In effect, they make an offer that is hard to refuse. They tend to put themselves last for the same reason. But the need to win love, not altruism, is their primary motive.

Pleasers like to blend into the group. They don't crave attention, fearing that close scrutiny will uncover their inadequacy and leave others disappointed in them. As a result, they take few interpersonal risks, rarely rock the boat, and behave obsequiously with authority.

Not hurting someone else's feelings is an important priority. Pleasers say things indirectly, use equivocating language, and avoid any hint of criticism. They are protective of other people's egos, probably because theirs are so fragile. They know how it feels to be crushed by a hostile word or gesture.

Pleasers are also tyrannized by ironclad rules of behavior. They feel that they should always be considerate, generous, courageous, and unselfish, and they are highly critical of any lapse in their behavior. Equally important, they should not be angry, resentful or jealous. Negative emotions, particularly anger, are dangerous because they may destroy a relationship or cause others to dislike them.

Because pleasers are so overfocused on meeting the expectations of others, they are usually out of touch with their own wants and needs. Their suffering usually results from believing that they haven't the right to assert for their personal happiness, and they allow other's opinions to unduly affect how they feel about themselves.

Help: *Step 1:* Accept that being liked is not the way to achieve personal happiness.

Step 2: Recognize that you must validate yourself and not always turn to others for approval.

Step 3: Acknowledge that you have the right to assert for your own needs and preferences.

EXAMPLE: Agreeable, enthusiastic Glynis is a twenty-nine-year-old data systems specialist for the telephone company. Popular among her friends, she has always been the kind of woman "you would take home to mother," someone who tries hard and plays by the rules.

For the past nine months, she has been in a relationship with Ted, another phone company employee. To the outsider, it appears an ideal match. Both of them like baseball, modern art, and nouvelle cuisine. Both find friendships important, value closeness with their families, and share similar preferences in people. Their main difficulty is sexual. Although their physical relationship started off well enough, after about six months Ted complained that their lovemaking was getting boring, that Glynis was not responsive enough. She just wasn't into it the way she had been.

Glynis took his criticism hard. She had always found it difficult to reach orgasm through coitus and was particularly sensitive to any put-down in the sexual arena. She automatically assumed Ted was right. It was her fault that their physical relationship was waning.

Glynis resolved to try harder. She read Masters and Johnson, bought body oil and a massage book. She made romantic dinners by candlelight; she suggested taking baths together; she even bought sexually explicit magazines. All the while she tried to be the perfect sexual partner, attuned to her lover's every need.

But rather than create a positive change, Glynis actually became less orgasmic. She experienced a decrease in sensation until it became almost impossible for her to reach climax. Ted's continued frustrations added to her confusion, and she began to wonder if there was something seriously wrong with her.

In desperation, Glynis sought out her friends for help. While exploring her feelings, she recognized that sex with Ted—except for the first few weeks, when everything was exciting and fresh—had never been satisfying for her. He was not sensual or gentle enough to make her feel comfortable, and she didn't trust him to give her the time to relax and feel her own sensations. Her latest efforts had backfired because of this distrust and because so much of her energy had been focused on pleasing him.

Glynis had buried her dissatisfactions, preferring not to deal with them, and hoped that the problem would work itself out. But even now, when she had become aware of her feelings once again, she still hesitated to express them. She feared that she would undercut Ted's masculinity and make him feel like a bad lover. She also didn't want to provoke a fight or have him respond with further accusations about her sexual inadequacy. Above all, she didn't want to lose his love.

Like most pleasers, Glynis's first impulse had been to blame herself and take responsibility for a situation that was clearly interactive. If there was blame to be assigned, it belonged to both of them. Ted's insensitivity to her sexual needs and her inability to voice those needs had produced the problem.

Despite her newly discovered insights, Glynis resolved to deal with the situation without talking directly to Ted. She didn't want to risk the feared consequences, and so she tried to change their lovemaking with nonverbal cues and such oblique comments as, "Let's have a nice evening by the fire." These merely confused and frustrated him further. Ted now felt that she was holding out on him. The crisis escalated until they stopped making love as a way to avoid conflict.

This situation tells us a great deal about pleasers. They are quick to blame themselves or to assume the rightness of the criticism directed at them. Their first impulse is to try harder, to make things right through the intensity and sincerity of their effort. They fear arousing the continued displeasure of their partner and will do almost anything to diffuse the anger or disapproval that surely must follow. Their knee-jerk reactions, which prevent them from accurately assessing the situation, result from their sense of themselves as deficient and unlovable. Glynis's difficulty in reaching orgasm highlighted that sense of inadequacy and made her doubly susceptible to criticism.

Her efforts to win back Ted's interest further distanced her from her body. She was so focused on pleasing him and performing to his satisfaction that she lost contact with herself. In making his needs primary, she had become less a lover than a servant of his pleasure, which only made the situation worse.

The desire to win approval and be loved is so powerful in pleasers that even when they recognize their limited responsibility for a problem, they are likely to avoid confronting the source. Glynis put off telling Ted precisely what he needed to know to save their physical relationship. Her fear of the consequences of speaking her mind resulted in greater difficulties.

PROFILE 3: THE MARTYR

Recognizable
Features:

Appears generally discontented and put upon by life; expects the worst.

Nurses and exaggerates suffering; feels sorry for self.

Shows awareness of own problems but not the problems of others.

Feels victimized by events and people.

Is stubborn; holds out.

Rarely admits to being wrong; blames others for difficulties; holds grudges.

Keeps silent, righteous anger inside; may appear brooding.

Envies those who have it better.

Attitudes and
Beliefs:

It is more important to be right than anything else.

I am judged and treated wrongly.

Most people have it better than me.

I am saddled with insolvable problems and demands from others.

People do things to me for which I am not responsible.

I don't have control over the events of my life.

I will be vindicated in the future.

People misunderstand me.

I can't change my fate.

Childhood:

Parents are critical and negative; child's identity is not affirmed.

Message to child: "You are not good enough."

Child's sense of self is compromised; feels undeserving of love and victimized; acts out victim role.

Work: Hard working, may be a workaholic.

Takes on too much, feels "righteous" resentment but will not set limits.

Chastises self for not living up to ideal employee image.

Tends to exaggerate problems on the job or how much work is required.

Feels underappreciated and unacknowledged.

Envies more successful co-workers.

Tends to go underground with gripes.

Has trouble asking for help.

Intimate Relationships: Collects grievances; keeps record of partner's wrongdoings; tends to be unforgiving.

Makes sacrifices and then feels resentful for having made them.

Expresses aggression and anger passively or indirectly (by being obstinate, oppositional, or negative).

Tends to blame partner for problems.

May pout or sulk rather than express hurt directly.

Doesn't take responsibility for own actions and feelings.

Sometimes acts spitefully.

Doesn't know how to ask for things; anger leaks out and alienates partner.

Sex:

Holds back from full experience of sexual expression and release.

Often takes inferior, subordinate role; may indulge in various masochistic practices from submissiveness to bondage.

Resentful when partner doesn't know what turns him or her on (though he or she hasn't made it known).

Agrees to sex when he or she doesn't want it and then feels manipulated.

Stingy lover; feels put upon by having to give to someone else; may withhold sex as punishment.

May feel anger that partner gets more enjoyment than he or she does.

Male/Female Ratio:

Larger percentage of females but more males than one might suspect, because they are more likely to keep these patterns hidden.

Analysis:

Martyrs are the classic masochists: long-suffering victims who feel embattled, put upon, and burdened by life. They are, in fact, failed pleasers. No matter how hard they have tried to meet other people's expectations, their attempts have always fallen short. Having been unsuccessful at getting love from their parents in childhood, they have a deep sense of being wronged that masks strong feelings of resentment. Their anger is bound up in grudges, churlishness, and self-hatred, but is rarely expressed directly. Martyrs are professional victims. They appear to embrace their suffering, always focusing on how they have been unjustly treated and paying little attention to their contribution to the problem. They are so caught up in having been wronged that they are usually more interested in a moral victory than a practical one.

Although martyrs tend to blame others for their misfortune, underneath they feel undeserving and worthless. This translates into the conviction that they have no right to pursue their own desires. Thus, to get satisfaction, they must put themselves in a flawlessly poor position. Only then do they feel justified in giving themselves what they need. Suffering not only evokes sympathy and attention but also supplies a moral victory of sorts. To be wronged assures one's own innocence and implies a righteousness of position. If they cannot get what they want, they can at least be right!

Martyrs live for future exoneration. "When the truth is known...," all the wrongs done to them will be exposed and they will be vindicated. In the meantime they resent their present circumstances but will do nothing to change them. They are mired in self-pity, although they make great efforts to keep it hidden. Their envy and criticism of others reflects their deep anger over the raw deal they feel they have gotten.

Help: *Step 1:* Acknowledge that suffering does not provide vindication, satisfaction, or power.

Step 2: Recognize fully the bad hand you have been dealt but also that you can choose new cards. You can exercise control over yourself and your circumstances.

Step 3: Forgive yourself for past offenses and wrongdoings.

EXAMPLE: Lucille, a dour-faced woman in her mid-forties with two children, works part-time as a teacher's aide to help meet household expenses. Her husband, Bill, is a machinist at a tool and die company, where he has been employed for nearly twenty years. They live in a suburban area, and their children, ages seven and nine, attend the same local primary school where Lucille works.

As a teenager, Lucille dreamed of becoming an actress, but when her break came, her parents vetoed her decision to accept a role with a small theater company. She married her husband on the rebound, never feeling he was the kind of man she deserved. She is particularly envious of her contemporaries whose marriages afford them the luxury of staying home and not working.

Recently, after much discussion, Lucille and Bill decided to send their kids to summer camp. They wanted to give them the kind of country experience that neither of them had enjoyed as children. But their decision created a financial strain; there was simply not enough money to cover all the camp costs. Lucille volunteered to find a second job. A friend who ran a small silk-screen business needed help. The hours were compatible with Lucille's responsibilities at school and it seemed like the perfect solution. However, about a week after she began working, she developed a rash on her hands from the heavy screening dyes. Gloves didn't seem to help. Her doctor gave her a topical ointment for relief and advised her to find other employment, but Lucille wouldn't hear of it. She kept working despite the pleas of her concerned husband and children.

Lucille thought, "I'm already making sacrifices by working two jobs, one more is not that big a deal. Besides, looking for another job is exhausting, and I'll probably never find one with compatible hours."

As her skin condition worsened, Lucille became more entrenched in her decision to stay at work. She absolutely refused to consider leaving. Meanwhile, she complained incessantly about her discomfort and made a big show of applying the prescribed ointment three times a day. She frequently reminded her children of what she was putting herself through just so they would have a good summer. She also began to cut back on her responsibilities at home. She stopped doing any household task that might exacerbate her condition. The kids picked up the slack, but they resented it and the tension in the family skyrocketed.

"Who wants to go to camp anyway? Why don't you just quit?" the younger one objected.

"I'm sick of hearing about what a sacrifice you're making for me," said the older one.

"Why can't you have any sympathy for me and appreciate what I'm doing for you instead of being such ingrates?" Lucille responded. But her words fell on deaf ears.

For Lucille, the situation was familiar. This was not the first time that she had acted selflessly, wanting only a little appreciation and gratitude for her sacrifices. But all she ever got was hostility, certainly no sympathy; worst of all, she got an "I couldn't care less" attitude from her children. Why were they so unappreciative? Why was she so misunderstood? Why was there no justice for the well-intentioned?

Martyrs always view themselves as victims of someone else's ill treatment. They see only honorable intentions in their actions, and they are always surprised and disturbed by the hostile responses they evoke.

But the intentions of martyrs are not exclusively honorable. They feel *compelled* to make sacrifices, which are less a reflection of love than a need to put themselves in insufferable positions to gain attention and appreciation. They persist even when they are clearly hurting themselves unnecessarily. Lucille could have sought other employment, but she convinced herself that no other job was possible. By continuing to work in an environment that was so obviously harmful to her health, she felt she was demonstrating what a truly altruistic and fine human being she was. While taking a second job for her children's benefit was a generous act, enduring physical discomfort raised her moral capital to new heights.

But the truly selfless individual does not draw attention to the sacrifice, does not make certain everyone else is aware of the noble intentions. Public appreciation has nothing to do with magnanimity of heart. Yet it has everything to do with martyrdom.

Unless they are truly saints, martyrs provoke a universally negative reaction. Because they are really looking for acknowledgment and appreciation, their acts of sacrifice appear manipulative, foolish, and unnecessary—hardly generous or bighearted.

PROFILE 4: THE AVOIDER

Recognizable Features: Two types: The *diverter* appears "speedy," engages in a "flurry of activity"; speaks rapidly in a pressured manner; and is prone to substance addiction, particularly alcohol and food (binge-eating). The *obscurer* lives in an emotional fog ("spaces out"); often expresses confusion; and acts without knowing why.

Cuts off feelings; has problems with their expression; shows disparity between what is felt and what is expressed (for example, "I'm angry at you" may be spoken in matter-of-fact tone).

Appears innocent and somewhat naive.

Puts things off until the last minute; often late or in a rush.

Has trouble making decisions.

Seems oblivious to upsetting events.

Suffers frequent psychosomatic problems—backaches, headaches, stomach troubles.

Shows tendency to phobic reactions.

Attitudes and   What I don't see can't hurt me.
Beliefs:
Things have a way of working out if you just let them run their course.

Don't disturb a difficult situation if you can help it.

I'll do it tomorrow when I really feel like it.

The world is a malignant and impossible place to live; it is best to retreat to a safe spot and come out only when necessary.

I can't make a real impact on my life, so why even try.

Childhood: Unresolvable conflicts in family system; all expression of feeling is avoided.

Message to child: "Emotions and conflict are better left unacknowledged."

Child experiences guilt for perceptions and deep-seated feelings; learns to distance self from emotions and become "socially blind."

Work: Is inconsistent: sometimes excellent, other times mediocre, reflecting ambivalence toward success.

Is apprehensive about any changes in workplace (procedure or personnel).

Has high rate of absenteeism.

Has problems with following through on tasks.

Tends to procrastinate on difficult assignments.

May sabotage excellent work at the last minute.

Is usually not found at the top levels of employment; prefers to avoid responsibility and headaches of high management.

Intimate Relationships: Avoids commitments and true intimacy; is cautious about entering new relationships; is uncommonly afraid of rejection.

Once involved, tends to stay ambivalent.

Often attracted to incompatible partners; closes eyes to negative traits.

May refuse to deal with inevitable conflicts in relationship; denies their existence; likely to refuse counseling.

Does not talk openly about self or share emotions; can't communicate heartfelt feelings.

Often stays in relationships to avoid loneliness or effort of finding a new partner.

Avoids authentic encounters.

Sex: May have trouble opening up to partner.

Tends toward long periods of abstinence.

Ambivalence toward relationship may appear indirectly in sexual arena. Possible modes of expression: withholding of sex; premature ejaculation; sexual indifference; sadistic and aggressive behavior toward partner.

Shies away from openly discussing sexual issues.

Male/ Female Ratio: Male-dominated type due to early sex-role training in the suppression of feelings—"big boys don't cry" syndrome.

Analysis: Raised in families where emotional conflicts and traumatic circumstances are denied as a way to cope with them, avoiders fear their deeper feelings and the intensity of human relationships. By closing off their emotional life, they feel a certain emptiness and flatness that is often masked by confusion, but they also sidestep a greater fear: encountering the strong feelings that lie beneath the surface. Unlike other EM types, who continually dredge up the past, avoiders will go to great lengths to keep their eyes shut to submerged anger and guilt, often paying a high price in the process. Their highspeed or spaced-out behavior distances them from these underlying currents.

Avoiders are largely unaware of their avoidance just as they are unaware of all deeper intention. They stay out of touch with themselves, which makes them particularly susceptible to the kind of self-sabotage that is provoked by unconscious fears and doubts (for example, showing up late for an important meeting).

Avoiders tend to be more passive than all the other profiles except perhaps the martyr. They wait for things to happen, rarely taking the initiative or squarely facing challenges. They have difficulty making choices and they are likely to put them off as long as possible. Their procrastination reflects their desire to evade the responsibility of making decisions and their fear that they will make the wrong ones. Although all Everyday Masochists are characterized by a certain amount of ambivalence, this is the hallmark of avoiders.

Because they are out of touch with themselves, they don't know what they want and are uncomfortable finding out. Committing to anything makes them feel trapped and produces panic. When they finally do commit, their decision is often poorly conceived and ill-timed.

Avoiders pay a high price for their evasion. They are subject to all the ills associated with denying feelings, including phobias, psychosomatic ailments such as rheumatoid arthritis, lower back pain, colitis, high levels of anxiety, and even sudden explosions of emotion.

Help:

Step 1: Wake up from the avoidant sleep and become aware of needs, desires, and feelings.

Step 2: Recognize that allowing yourself to feel will not produce catastrophic consequences.

Step 3: Acknowledge that inaction is creating the very problems action is assumed to create.

EXAMPLE: A youthful-looking man in his late thirties, Hank was a teacher who had drifted into carpentry when the school district's budget was slashed. He had met Debby on the ski slopes, and by nightfall they were already sharing a room. Though friends predicted that the relationship would never last, Hank ignored their prognostications as he had ignored their other advice. He was uncertain, however, that he wanted a long-term relationship and was equally confused about his feelings for Debby. If she hadn't pushed, he would have been content to remain on a dating basis for quite some time.

But Debby had been insistent, and so they moved into an apartment the night they celebrated their six-month anniversary. They got along well, and when Debby became pregnant with their first child, they talked about getting married. Hank was ambivalent about it. He wasn't sure he wanted the official sanction of the state, and he was less certain that he wanted to be a husband. Privately he thought, "I'm not positive I want to stay with this woman for the rest of my life. If we marry, I'll be trapped."

Each time Debby brought up the subject, Hank would ask for more time, until she finally just gave up trying. They never married, although they lived as husband and wife and raised their child together.

After three years, Debby decided to return to school to get a graduate degree. She was at home fewer hours and more of the household and child-rearing responsibilities fell to Hank. He didn't mind. School would be over in a few years, and then things would get back to normal.

But as time went on, he and Debby saw less and less of each other. They hardly talked about anything except the arrangements for child-care, and their sexual relationship waned. They began to have little blowups over inconsequential matters, though they always managed to avoid a real fight. As a rule, Debby put school business first, the relationship a clear second. Hank tried hard not to acknowledge what was happening. He continued to rationalize the situation, believing that it was only temporary. He refused to let himself feel resentment, anger, or abandonment. Things would get back to normal soon. He just had to wait it out.

Then Debby came home with shocking news. She was involved with another man. Though the affair had been going on only a short time, Debby was unwilling to give it up. She felt the emptiness in her relationship with Hank and craved the warmth and attention her new intimacy provided. Hank was stunned. That night he wandered around town aimlessly, wondering what to do. All this time he had been patient, accepting her absence and disinterest without pressuring or resenting her. Now she was clearly abusing his goodwill by giving her precious free time to another person.

All the anger that Hank had suppressed over the years began to surface. One hostile thought after another bombarded him. He felt a hatred inside himself that both surprised and scared him. He could barely keep it under control. Then he began attacking himself with demeaning thoughts about his adequacy and his blindness to the obvious. When he returned home, he was so choked up with feeling that he couldn't talk.

The next morning, as he looked into his child's unsuspecting eyes, tears started rolling down his face. He felt betrayed. Scenes of previous hurt from the archives of his memory sent shivers through his body. He remembered an incident at age ten when his mother had left him, and he recalled a painful experience of failure in college. The tap was open. It was all streaming forth.

Yet one question kept recurring. He had been patient, suppressing his feelings, not making demands so that everything would turn out all right. But his strategy had backfired badly. How could it have happened when he had such noble intentions?

Avoiders often rationalize their actions by claiming they are only being patient or thoughtful. The fuller truth is that they are afraid to confront the uncomfortable reality that faces them. When Hank felt Debby's growing disinterest, he might have faced the situation squarely. Instead, he ignored the problem until it became a crisis. He could do this by distancing himself from his feelings. As long as he remained unaware of his resentment and hurt, he did not have any reason to act.

Like all avoiders, Hank was afraid of asserting for himself, taking a risk, and making demands. He didn't feel he could stand up to Debby's reaction. As it was, he felt guilty about not marrying her. If he called attention to her indifferent behavior, perhaps she would leave him altogether. Yet through his passivity, Hank created the very circumstance he had hoped to prevent. Without intervention, the problem simply escalated until it could no longer be ignored. By that time, it was just too late.

Chapter **Four**

A Dictionary of Masochism

God defend me from myself.

MONTAIGNE

We have already seen numerous ways in which Everyday Masochists defeat themselves and suffer unnecessarily. The variety of psychological traps and tortures is endless. In my clinical practice over the years I have seen the full spectrum of EM behaviors and attitudes. Drawing on my observations and the work of the cognitive behavioral psychologists, I have collected some of these self-inflicted tyrannies and created a catalog of woe, a dictionary of Everyday Masochism.

I have divided these traps into four different types: binds, sabotages, torments, and musterbations. I do not mean to suggest that this list is all-inclusive. What I present here is a listing of the more common forms of gratuitous suffering engaged in by the Everyday Masochist. Following each of the traps is an exercise (or exercises) tailored to the problem that will be of immediate help to the reader. Additional exercises are presented in Chapter 9.

BINDS

These are obstructions, impediments to satisfaction that are self-imposed, sometimes unconsciously. A bind is a no-win situation in which all acknowledged alternatives lead to failure or frustration. It is like locking yourself in a closet and slipping the key under the door.

Binds are usually the result of ambivalence, guilt, the failure to see choices where they exist, and conflict between what one *should* and what one *wants* to do. To the outsider they make no sense at all. Why would someone want to put himself in a no-exit position unnecessarily? But to the Everyday Masochist, the bind is not a choice. It is merely an unfortunate circumstance that can't be helped.

Here are some typical examples:

> When Natalie is not in an intimate relationship, she feels miserable and lonely. She thinks to herself, "If only I had a man, all my troubles would be over. . . . It seems like everyone else in the world has someone but me. . . . Life is empty if you can't share it with someone else." But once in a relationship, Natalie feels no better. Forgetting her previous longing, she focuses only on how much she must accommodate to her partner. She feels trapped and suffocated and longs for her freedom.
>
> *   *   *
>
> When Phyllis doesn't set limits on her mother's involvement in her life, she feels overrun and resentful of the daily phone calls, complaints, and demands. When she does set limits (even politely), she feels guilty and wrong: "I'm a bad daughter"; "She'll never forgive me"; "She won't ever like me again."
>
> *   *   *
>
> Ted wants a leaner, more muscular body that he can parade on the beach. But he won't go to the aerobics classes that would develop and trim his torso. Why? He's

embarrassed about how he will appear in his workout clothes.

*   *   *

Monica is planning to go to law school and must take the necessary aptitude tests. She's very anxious on exam day and her scores are uncharacteristically low. She feels disappointed and inadequate. "I'm just not cut out for law," she tells herself, "I'm not smart enough to make it through." Some months later she takes the tests again and this time her marks are outstanding. Rather than feel pleased, she castigates herself, "This proves I haven't been living up to my full potential as a student. My course grades should have been higher all through college."

*   *   *

When Jack is passive, cautious, and undemonstrative in sexual encounters, he feels inadequate as a man and not much of a lover. When he pushes himself to be sexually assertive and take a more active role, he feels guilty for being lascivious and indecent.

*   *   *

Martha feels disappointed in her sexual partner, who fails to take the initiative and assume a more dominant role. When he gets the message and behaves more aggressively, she feels threatened and violated.

*   *   *

When Richard is busy with work and daily chores, he dreams of relaxed days with nothing to do but smell the flowers. When he finds himself with a "free day," he can think of nothing but work.

Exercise: Reclaiming Choices

As we now know, most Everyday Masochists squander their choices by failing to acknowledge them. They accomplish this by semantic manipulation. They substitute the word *can't* for *want* to suggest that they have no choice in the matter. "I don't want to put in the work necessary to pass the test" is converted to "I can't pass." "I am unwilling to forgive him" becomes "I just can't forgive him," and so forth. The following paper and pencil task addresses this problem.

Step 1: Compile a list of at least fifteen "I can'ts" from every part of your life—family, relationships, work, sex. Examples: "I can't ever get to work on time"; "I can't deal with my boss"; "I can't take control of my life."

Step 2: Substitute "I don't want to" or "I choose not to" for every "I can't." For example, "I can't get to work on time" becomes "I choose not to get to work. . . ."

Step 3: Look over the second list. How does the word substitution change the meaning of the sentences? What is your reaction to the rephrasing? How many of the sentences are more accurate in their new form? What conclusions can be drawn about your "can'ts"?

SABOTAGES

These are maneuvers in which one's long-term or best interests are undermined by an action or series of actions that bring destructive consequences. Generally, the sabotage looks innocent enough—an inadvertent accident or a simple error—but on closer examination, a primary, more powerful motivation can be detected. The individual is usually only partially aware of this unconscious motive and, in fact, may be resistant to acknowledging it.

In every case of sabotage what appears to be a random or accidental act is an expression of a deep need or fear. To understand or change undermining behaviors, one must have an awareness of these driving motives. In the examples below, the underlying forces are identified.

Failing to Finish

Suzanne, a doctoral candidate in psychology, is the first person in her family to seek a graduate degree. In the first three years of school she does exceptionally well, getting good grades and positive evaluations from her teachers. But she is wary of the task that awaits her. Like every psychology student, she must write a dissertation. At heart she doesn't think she's up to it.

Her work goes smoothly, but as she nears completion she finds herself getting bogged down. She spends long periods struggling over minor points. When her deadline approaches, she files for an extension, yet even with the additional time she still can't finish. She becomes increasingly critical of her writing and finds numerous other "flaws" that require her to re-work whole sections of the text. In fact, her task becomes so confusing and the demands so unbearable that she finally decides to scrap the whole project. In doing so she gives up three years of excellent academic effort and a promising new profession.

COMMENT: Suzanne starts off with a flourish, but the closer she gets to the end, the more obstacles she puts in her path. Completing her dissertation would subject her academic efforts to one final scrutiny, and her feelings of self-doubt are so strong that she imagines a humiliating ending. Yet she is an excellent student. Like all Everyday Masochists, she minimizes her strengths and focuses on her weaknesses. The result is a distorted vision of herself that weakens confidence and actually encourages failure. By bowing out before the final curtain, Suzanne throws away her academic career rather than risk the possibility that her efforts will be judged substandard.

Procrastination

Trish has worked for two years as an executive secretary for a lawyer who has consistently praised her work. After six months she expected at least a token raise, but none was forthcoming. At Christmas she received a small bonus and a bottle of toilet water but no raise. Meanwhile, her responsibilities and work load were gradually increasing.

Trish complained to her husband who urged her to assert herself. She resolved to ask for more money, but as the months went by, she never found the "right time." Whenever she determined that "this will be the day," her boss seemed preoccupied, overworked, or in a bad mood, and she remained silent. Recently he has been talking about cost cutting measures and Trish is despairing about ever getting a pay increase. Her procrastination has cost her emotionally and financially.

COMMENT: Procrastination is one of the most common forms of sabotage. As you might expect, the avoider has made a life-style of it. But it is found in the other masochistic types as well. The perfectionist puts things off because he fears his performance will be less than flawless. The pleaser doubts her adequacy. The martyr delays as a protest against something she did not want to do but could not refuse. There are as many reasons for procrastinating as there are procrastinators. Everyday Masochists believe they need the pressure of the last minute to force them into action. But most of the time delaying only compromises the best efforts of the individual and creates needless pressure.

Trish's experience is typical. She puts off asking for a raise until it becomes an almost impossible task. Other examples of this are: the delayed dental checkup that now feels like an appointment for major surgery; the short note to an old friend that "becomes longer" with each passing day.

Fear of Failure

Raymond is giving the keynote address at the Rotary Club annual dinner. He has never spoken in front of a large gathering of people before and is quite anxious. Time after time, he delivers his meticulously prepared speech to his wife and children, rehearsing it while driving to and from work and in bed before sleeping. Despite these endless practice sessions, his anxiety continues unabated, and he spends several sleepless nights worrying about how things could go wrong. On the day of the dinner, he looks in his appointment book to see when he is expected. He reads "8:00 P.M.," but when he arrives, he finds no one around. The maintenance man informs him that everyone left shortly after seven when the scheduled speaker failed to show up.

COMMENT: Raymond's behavior looks like an unfortunate slipup. He misreads the time and arrives too late. It could happen to anyone. In *Psychopathology of Everyday Life*, Freud reminds us that errors are rarely accidental: They have deeper purposes that can generally be identified by probing under the surface. In this case, Raymond made a mistake that is uncharacteristic of so methodical a person—he is usually precise about dates and times. Why an error now and particularly one that had him arriving later rather than earlier?

Raymond was very nervous about giving his speech. He worried about doing poorly, and no amount of practice seemed to alleviate his anxiety. His fear of failure was the driving force behind his mistake. By unconsciously misreading the time, he managed to avoid a highly charged situation without falling on his face.

Fear of Success

Jennifer is a young ballet dancer with a promising career. This year, for the first time, she will dance in several solo pieces. But she is wary of her new role and somewhat uncertain about whether she is ready to devote as much energy to dance as her premiere position will require. While painting her apartment the day before her big debut, she falls off a ladder and severely twists her ankle. She is forced out of the performance and is laid up for the rest of the season.

COMMENT: Is Jennifer's "accident" unintentional or purposeful? The facts of the situation are suggestive. She is ambivalent about her success, uncertain as to whether she is ready, and her accident occurs just before she steps into the limelight. Falling is out of character for a person with such great physical agility. The fall creates a situation in which she is literally "not ready to perform."

It all fits together in psychological logic. The missing element is her fear of success. This is the flip side of fear of failure, but unlike the first situation, here the Everyday Masochist is scared that, once successful, she will have to live up to continuing expectations of success. Her fall represents an unconscious attempt to avoid success without actually having to confront her ambivalence.

The Confessional

Barbara works in the advertising department of a large, international agency. She meets with her boss on a monthly basis to discuss the status of her projects and make future plans. At their last meeting, in response to a general question regarding her present assignment, Barbara began this way: "To tell you the truth, I haven't been doing as good a job as I should. I couldn't concentrate last week and got sidetracked on a few minor details. I don't think I did one thing that was truly productive. It cost me a lot of time. I'm really quite disappointed in my performance since we last met."

COMMENT: Barbara inappropriately begins the meeting by pointing out her own failings and disclosing her disappointment in herself. Her statements have the flavor of a "confessional." She is compelled to reveal feelings that are both compromising and irrelevant to the meeting at hand—a discussion of the progress of the project. She appears to be asking for sympathy or absolution, neither of which is appropriate. Her admissions only serve to create a negative impression in her boss's eyes and subvert her standing as a competent worker.

Are Barbara's negative judgments even accurate? A statement such as "I don't think I did one thing that was truly productive" suggests that she has a distorted view of her actions. It is hard to believe in someone who does not believe in herself.

Dexifying: Defending, EXplaining, JustIFYING

Leslie's roommate, a stewardess, repeatedly asks her for rides to the airport. Leslie is inconvenienced by these favors but finds it very difficult to say "no." After several months of putting herself out, she decides to refuse. But instead of simply saying "no," the interaction goes like this:

ROOMMATE: Could you give me a ride to the airport tomorrow?

LESLIE: I really don't see how I can because I have to go grocery shopping before work.

ROOMMATE: Oh, that's no problem. I can pick up groceries when I get back, or you could get them tomorrow morning. The house is pretty well stocked right now anyway.

LESLIE: Yeah, but I also have to pick up my suits at the dry cleaners.

ROOMMATE: Well, couldn't that wait? You really don't need them till next week anyway.

LESLIE: I suppose so. But if I give you a lift, I'll get stuck in airport traffic like last week.

ROOMMATE: No problem. We can leave a few minutes earlier.

LESLIE: Well, I guess so, as long as we leave enough time.

COMMENT: Rather than saying "no" without elaboration, Leslie feels she must justify her behavior. She doesn't want to appear selfish or unfriendly, and she is afraid of provoking her roommate's anger or disapproval. But in explaining why she can't go to the airport, she leaves herself vulnerable to argument and manipulation. She has undermined the strength of her refusal by weighing it down with justification.

This is a common masochistic sabotage that I describe with the acronym "dexify." When individuals defend, explain, or justify, they are unnecessarily supporting the reasons for their decision and giving others the opportunity to rebut their rationale. The stronger position is an unadorned "no," perhaps with a softening statement such as "That won't work for me." Neither of these responses lends itself to challenge. They imply, "The doors on this decision are closed. It is not open for discussion." Such a position is difficult for Everyday Masochists to take because they are overfocused on the wish to be liked and the need to avoid criticism.

Exercises:

The exercises that follow will help you identify feelings, sensations, and hidden motives that may cause you to act against your perceived interests.

1. Awareness Continuum

Step 1: Find a quiet place and give yourself about thirty minutes to do the exercise. Lie on your back with your knees raised and breathe deeply into your abdomen. Close your eyes. As soon as you feel your back sinking to the floor, go on to the next step.

Step 2: Pay attention to the sensations in your body. Notice your breathing. Is it deep or shallow? Labored or easy? Regular or arrhythmic? When you breathe, do you feel movement in your chest? What about your abdomen? Does it feel harder to inhale or exhale? Are you taking in air exclusively through your nose? These are the kinds of things to be looking for—small details, subtle cues, minor changes.

Step 3: Now say what you observe out loud in a continual stream of awareness. Use the introductory words *I notice.* . . . It should sound something like this: "I notice tension across my chest"; "I notice my right hand itches"; "I notice I feel sleepy"; "I notice my legs feel heavy"; "I notice I'm self-conscious about doing this." Keep going for as long as you can, up to twenty minutes at least. By the time you're done, you'll be aware of sensations you hardly knew existed.

You'll also notice that you've slowed down quite a bit. To observe and feel these subtle physical sensations requires a different pace than what is needed to make dinner or go to the office. It's like the difference between touring the countryside by car or going on foot. The latter allows you to see details you couldn't possibly recognize while cruising at 55 miles per hour.

Step 4: Begin to note your emotions and moods. What are you feeling? Sadness? Anxiety? Anger? Identify these out loud, including any absence of emotion. Now ask yourself from which part of your body your feelings seem to emanate. Is it your stomach, diaphragm, chest? Breathe into that part of your body. What is the effect? Now hold your breath and tighten all the muscles in your torso. What is the effect?

Step 5: Take three deep cleansing breaths, open your eyes, and sit up slowly. How do you feel now as compared with when you started the exercise? Walk around the room slowly with the same level of awareness you had a few moments ago. What have you discovered?

2. Synthesizing

Step 1: Repeat Step 1 of the previous exercise.

Step 2: Think about an important decision you need to make. It might be whether to change jobs, begin a new relationship, or buy a house. Any significant decision will do. What does your head say about your choice? Weigh the pros and cons and see where you stand. Do you feel comfortable with a purely rational choice?

Step 3: Repeat Step 2 of the Awareness Continuum. When you have put your full attention on your physical sensations, ask yourself what your body says about the decision. Imagine making a particular choice. Does your body tense in response? Does your breathing stay relaxed? Do you feel anxious? Do you sense any changes in temperature? What other signals is your body sending out?

Step 4: What does your heart say about the matter? Do you feel joy, letdown, or no feeling at all? Now see what your gut reaction is. Do you get a sickening feeling in your stomach? Do you feel unburdened and lighter? What other sensations are you aware of?

Step 5: Is there a conflict between your body and mind? If the answer is "no," end the exercise here. You are "unified" in your decision to take a particular course of action. If the answer is "yes," which are you inclined to follow? Why? What has happened in the past when you have followed this inclination?

Step 6: Rather than allow one part of you to predominate, make a new decision that synthesizes the concerns of both your body and mind. Feel your reaction to such a choice.

TORMENTS

These are patterns of making oneself miserable by thinking or acting in ways that thwart satisfaction and produce feelings of frustration, self-contempt, and hopelessness. When it comes to chronic self-persecution, Everyday Masochists are peerless.

In some ways, the process of tormenting oneself resembles the senseless behavior of the flagellants who marched through the towns and countryside of medieval Europe whipping themselves furiously with leather straps. Through the imposition of pain, they sought absolution from their sins.

The self-inflictions of the Everyday Masochist are, of course, psychological, not physical, and only partially motivated by the need for exoneration. Yet they have the same blind, irrational quality. Sometimes they are the result of distorted thought processes that are so embedded in the individual's way of thinking that he or she hardly knows of their existence. At other times they reflect a compulsive need to reenact or reexperience old feelings of inadequacy or hurt.

Torments have virtually no redeeming value, but their chronic nature makes them hard to change. They are not the exclusive property of those high on the EM scale either. Anyone may indulge in them, but Everyday Masochists, because of their low self-esteem and unconscious guilt, are naturally inclined. Indeed, they do not surrender their leather straps easily.

Calamitizing

When you expect the worst, imagine disaster, anticipate catastrophe, you are "calamitizing." An individual with a stomach pain believes he has abdominal cancer. A well-regarded businesswoman loses a sale and expects she will be fired. A mother on the beach thinks her ten-year-old has drowned when he has only been on a long line at the refreshment stand. At its worst, calamitous thinking can scare the daylights out of you and create a panic reaction. At best, it is a slow torture in which the most unlikely and horrendous possibility is gradually woven into a cloak of reality.

Many calamitous thoughts begin with the phrase "what if." The words themselves have an incendiary quality. *What if* that phone ringing is someone calling to tell me my husband has had a heart attack? *What if* I commit myself to this relationship and she leaves me? *What if* I get sick and can no longer work? The possibilities are endless, and the morbid mind can have a field day tormenting itself with reckless imaginings.

Salting the Wound

Everyday Masochists seek out troubling information and use it to salt old wounds and sensitivities. Examples:

A man is at a party also attended by his former girlfriend whom he still cares about. During the entire evening he watches her out of the corner of his eye, feeling miserable as she flirts with every man in the room.

A woman learns that her husband is having an affair. She demands to know the details of his sexual relationship. After he tells her, she feels worse than before.

A father learns that his son has been killed in an automobile accident. Every day he goes back to the street corner where it took place and re-creates the scene in his mind. Although he is shaken and angered each time, he continues to return.

Salting the wound is a little like touching your tongue to a decayed tooth. Although you experience a jolt of pain when you do it, you repeat the action again and again. You know what will happen, of course, but that doesn't stop you. Strangely, the more pain you feel, the more you are drawn to the tooth. Something in the experience of suffering is terribly compelling.

No single motivation can explain this intentional torment. Sometimes, as in the case of the father, it is to drive home a reality that cannot otherwise be accepted. At other times, it is to titillate and test one's ability to bear pain. At still other times, it is to relieve guilt feelings through suffering. Whatever the motive, the process is anything but pleasant and appears incomprehensible to outsiders and sometimes to masochists themselves.

Screening

This most common of EM torments describes a thought process in which individuals *screen* out the positive aspects of their experience and magnify the negative. Suppose, for example, I go for a job interview. In the hour during which I answer questions, there are perhaps three or four minutes when I lose my concentration and appear less than certain of myself. The rest of the time I do quite well. If I dwell on those few moments, exaggerating their impact and importance, and filter out all that was positive in my presentation, I am screening.

Another example: A teacher is evaluated by his supervisor, who gives him excellent marks on motivation, attitude, organization, and communication skills. The supervisor also mentions his lateness as an area that needs improvement. Despite the overwhelmingly positive nature of the assessment, the teacher concludes that his supervisor thinks he's not giving enough time to the job.

Screening is a form of tunnel vision. One loses perspective on the whole field and takes in only a part of it. And that part, predictably, is what the individual is most afraid of perceiving. Thus a person who feels inadequate and afraid of criticism will be sensitive to anything that appears remotely critical. An anxious or phobic individual will see grave danger where others note only minor risk.

When the negative is pulled out of context and isolated from the larger situation (where it is only one factor among many), it is ripe for distortion. Its frequency and importance can be easily misrepresented and used for self-torment. A stage actor who had won many dramatic awards once joked that despite his successes, he would always think of himself as the man who had flubbed a line while performing in front of the Queen of England.

Discounting

In the converse of screening, one *discounts* or underplays the positive aspects of an experience without necessarily exaggerating the negative. Examples:

Someone compliments my guitar playing, and I say to myself, "What does he know; he's not a musician."

I get a high grade in a college physics class and think, "It means nothing. The course was a gut."

The first month on the job, I double my sales quota and chalk it up to beginner's luck.

In all three situations I downplay my achievements and prevent myself from enjoying the satisfaction that goes with them.

Discounting is a form of personal devaluation. If I run a marathon, for example, then it can't be too difficult a task in the first place. If a woman shows an interest in me, then she must not be very desirable. Such distorted thinking inspired Groucho Marx to coin the classic phrase, "I wouldn't join a club that would have me as a member." His remark is the ultimate self–put down. Whatever I do or have is *less good* than what others do or have.

By continually devaluing their accomplishments, Everyday Masochists diminish themselves and ensure that their self-esteem remains low. Like screening, discounting is a way of distorting feedback to arrive at the same conclusion: "I am inadequate."

Grouching

This torment has many synonyms: bitching, complaining, griping, and bellyaching to name a few. All describe the same process of expressing in words and tone one's feelings of discontent, uneasiness, grief, and pain. Grouching never makes anyone feel better. In fact, the process usually foments greater agitation as one complaint sets off another.

Grouching gives the appearance of really doing something when it is actually a substitute for taking action. People who grouch are looking for sympathy, validation, and relief. They are not looking to change. If they were, they would not waste so much time talking endlessly about how bad things are. For many Everyday Masochists, grouching is a substitute for expressing anger directly. Since aggressive statements might provoke retaliation, disapproval, or dislike, grouching is a safer alternative. No one is threatened by a complainer, but by the same token, no one is influenced by one. An Arab proverb puts it simply: "The dogs bark, but the caravan moves on."

Globalizing

From a single piece of "negative" information, the individual draws a conclusion that is false and overgeneralized. A beginning novelist, for example, receives a bad review and concludes that this is the beginning of the end, no one will appreciate the novel, sales will be poor, and the publisher will surely reject the next offering.

Globalizing is the name of the game. This is accomplished by overreading the meaning of a particular event and exaggerating the consequences. Thus, one bad quarter is seen as evidence of impending bankruptcy, several sliced drives mean "I should never have taken up golf," and getting turned down for a date proves that "no one will ever go out with me."

Globalizing has no basis in reality. The conclusions drawn represent fears, not actualities, but they can have the effect of hard facts in influencing behavior. A young patient of mine was turned down by a woman with whom he wanted to have an affair. Misreading her rejection, he interpreted what happened to mean that no woman could love him. He then refused to engage in any social or sexual activity, feeling that further rejection would be too painful to bear. The truth of the matter, he later found out, was that the woman had recently undergone an abortion and was hesitant about entering into sexual involvements with any man.

Word Processing

Everyday Masochists perform their own kind of word processing. They transform "wants" into "shoulds," making chores out of tasks they once actually wanted to do. Then they resent the new burden. One of my patients in his mid-forties told me that he was tired of being a "flab collector" and wanted to tone up his body once and for all. He set up a program at the local gym, but after several weeks of working out, he began to lose interest.

"I should get on those Nautilus machines," he groaned, "but I never find the time. It's one more thing I have to do."

"You have to?" I said to him. "I thought you wanted to." He had converted desire into obligation and in the process lost touch with his original intentions.

When "I want" becomes "I should," the resentment and opposition begin. "I want to learn new job skills" is a positive thought, but "I should learn new skills" is a wearisome idea. "I want to be physically healthy" is a constructive wish until it becomes a chore that must be done. Then all motivation fades away.

What is the motive behind these self-defeating conversions? Everyday Masochists easily lose contact with their original wants, often feeling selfish and guilty for asserting them. In contrast, something that must or should be done is seen as justifiable, although it is aggravating and feels like yet another burden. Put simply, EMs are more comfortable following self-imposed rules, no matter how arduous, than asserting their wants.

Lamenting

This is the process of reliving past experiences, not for the sake of learning from them but to torment oneself over failures of courage or foresight. Examples:

A young man leaves a management training program because he doesn't feel ready to take a high-powered administrative job. Many months later, feeling confused and uncertain of the future, he dwells obsessively on his decision: "If only I had stuck it out."

A couple in their mid-thirties is having sexual problems. Neither is able to talk frankly about the situation. Gradually, their sexual difficulties undermine other aspects of their relationship and they separate. Years later they still lament about what might have been if only they had confronted their problems.

A middle-aged woman with three children and a new divorce is filled with bitter remorse over her decision twenty years earlier to sacrifice her law career for marriage.

The key phrase in this process is "if only." *If only* I had been more committed. *If only* we had challenged our fears. *If only* I had gone to school then. It is normal to have some feelings of regret. At one point or another, any significant, painful experience—particularly a loss—elicits an "if only" response. The difference is that for Everyday Masochists, lamenting is a life-style. It continues long after the regretted event and focuses the person on the past so that he or she cannot fully live in the present. It is an avoidance mechanism that keeps individuals from taking charge of their lives.

Measuring Down

Everyday Masochists expend a lot of mental energy comparing themselves to other people. Particularly in new situations, almost as if by reflex, they measure themselves against others even when those circumstances are not competitive. What they are really after is reassurance. They want to confirm that they are the equals of anyone else in the room, a fact about which they have some doubt. The problem is that EMs contrast the social facade of strangers against a biased appraisal of themselves. They know their own shortcomings all too well; in fact, they exaggerate them. The other person, by contrast, is assumed to be an unblemished paragon of virtue and accomplishment. The result is an unfair comparison that leaves them on the short end. They are always measuring down.

A patient of mine who worked for a large international oil cartel ran this torment on himself continually. Every time he attended a meeting he measured himself against all the men in the room. He made comparisons of physical attractiveness, intelligence, verbal ability, and what he called "natural authority." Invariably, he came out feeling diminished. Even when he saw one of his "competitors" blunder, he dismissed the occurrence as an anomaly. He always gave the benefit of the doubt to others while judging himself harshly. His double standard was his undoing.

Another patient of mine who was also a psychologist used a similar version of measuring down. When she was stymied by a difficult client, she would say to herself, "I shouldn't be seeing this person. If he were in therapy with A, he wouldn't be stuck like this and everyone would be much better off." Her comparison produced two ill effects: first, it reinforced her doubts about herself, making her a less effective therapist; and second, it diverted her from the issue of how to move through the therapeutic impasse.

Masquerading

Some researchers estimate that two out of every five successful people feel they are fakes. Even famous people are susceptible. Richard Burton, shortly before his death, remarked that "inside he felt he was just a poor boy from a Welsh mining town, and did not really deserve all his fame." Such feelings are considered normal when individuals are in transition—for example, when stepping into a new job or unfamiliar social role.

But Everyday Masochists are birds of another feather. Their belief that they are impostors is not limited to short periods of change; it is a relative constant that remains throughout their lives. And no matter how much they achieve, their doubts hang on. They discount their successes by minimizing them, seeing them as aberrations, or believing that they have been gained through luck or charm rather than ability.

An Olympic swimmer I know confided that he was not really champion material. Although he had won dozens of regional races and was an All-American, he felt his success was the result of hard work and very little natural ability. "The other guys are the real talents. I've just pushed myself hard and managed to swim above my capabilities."

A marketing executive for a Silicon Valley computer firm engaged in the same kind of thinking. He had almost single-handedly tripled his young company's sales in nine months, but he still felt he was a fraud who had just showed up at the right moment. No amount of data, logic, or disputation could convince him otherwise.

Some studies show that individuals who feel like charlatans are the first in their families to attain high levels of achievement. Other research indicates that the individual comes from a family in which another sibling was seen as smarter. Still other theories maintain that diminishing one's achievements is a way of avoiding guilt for surpassing the accomplishments of a parent.

Any number of childhood scenarios can create the self-doubt that underlies this torment. As long as children are repeatedly taught to believe that their value and ability are questionable, they will come to feel that they are masquerading as successes.

Personalizing

When individuals interpret the actions of others as having specific meaning for them, the process is called "personalizing." Individuals with high EM scores always personalize in the negative. Examples:

If a masochist gives a party and a friend tells her that he can't attend, she's likely to think he's refusing because he doesn't like her.

If her husband says one evening that he doesn't feel like making love, she suspects she's done something to alienate him.

If a friend complains about how stingy most people are, she imagines he's talking about her.

In all three situations, the masochist assumes without corroboration that an individual's actions are intended to send a personal message. Simpler explanations are more likely. The invitee had a prior commitment. The husband was tired or preoccupied. The friend was talking in general terms.

A specific form of personalizing typical of many EM types is "projecting criticism," seeing reprimands where they don't exist. Examples:

A tennis coach calls over one of his players to give her a few tips on how to improve her service. The athlete feels humiliated and leaves the court in tears.

A patron in a restaurant tells his waiter to speed things up;

he needs to make an eight o'clock curtain. The waiter takes his remark as an attack on his competence.

A spouse complains about the high cost of living. Her mate suspects she's commenting on his failure as a provider.

We are all guilty from time to time of taking things personally when they are not so intended, but EMs make a full-time job of it. Since they are always looking to others for clues about their value, they are prone to "overread" the significance of vague or ambiguous statements.

Federal Offenses and Other Major Crimes

Carol gets a parking ticket and beats herself up about it for the next twenty-four hours. David misses his exit on the freeway, arrives a few minutes late for a meeting, and berates himself for his inattention and stupidity. Harriet burns the vegetables at a dinner party and feels embarrassed all evening. Everyday Masochists make federal crimes out of inconsequential errors and flagellate themselves long after the event.

Anyone who has ever engaged in "federal offenses"—and who hasn't—knows that there is an aspect of punishment in this torment. Having made a mistake, the person tries to atone for his or her sins by refusing to let the matter go. Absolution is earned through misery. Yet perhaps there is a practical goal in mind as well: to make oneself feel so bad that repeated offenses will be eliminated. In either case, the torment is unsuccessful. Excessive self-blame doesn't provide atonement or prevent future errors. It just makes life a lot more aggravating than it has to be.

Mental Movies

Everyday Masochists frequently dwell on past experiences of humiliation, shame, and failure. They dredge up these painful moments and torture themselves with mental movies of their embarrassment and disgrace. Sometimes these thoughts are triggered by similar events in their current lives. At other times they seem evoked by fears and doubts. Often they appear in dreams or fantasies.

Although the process is similar to lamenting in its focus on past events, the latter is chiefly an experience of regret ("If only"). "Mental movies" has nothing to do with remorse. It is simply the condition of "bumming oneself out" by reliving degrading moments.

A handball instructor who had trained many top-flight players told me the story of a well-known professional who had lost badly in his last match with his arch rival. The instructor related how this player spent many sleepless nights reliving the feelings of humiliation and exaggerating his poor play. When the time came to face his competition again, he was so "psyched out" that he canceled, claiming ill health as an excuse.

A business consultant who scored high on the EM scale related how he had given a pilot presentation to the sales managers of a large American corporation. It went poorly and the company decided not to hire him. Over and over he reviewed the experience in his mind, making himself miserable and feeling like an incompetent failure. "It was a ritual I had to perform," he said.

By taking us back to past agonies and mortifications, mental movies set the stage for continued failure. They introduce painful images that cannot help but undermine future efforts. Old failure has a way of creating new failure. Humiliations that remain with us undermine our self-esteem and keep us looking backward instead of to the future. Everyday Masochists feel unable to let the troubling past fade into the background. They hold onto it the way someone might clutch a treasured memento. One of my patients summarized it thus,

"Time heals all wounds but mine. I would feel empty without my memories, no matter how unpleasant."

Garbage Collecting

It's a beautiful day, the sun is shining, the sky is azure blue, the air feels brisk, and you're sitting inside thinking about everything that's going wrong in your life. The clutch on your car is on its last legs, you can't pay your bills, your oldest son has been rejected from college, and your roof leaks.

Dwelling on all the aggravations in your life is what I call "garbage collecting." Everyone has problems. No one can deny that contemporary life is stressful. But overwhelming oneself with a laundry list of irritations and vexations is a good way to crush one's spirit and initiative. Everyday Masochists like to play in the garbage.

A variant of this torment, practiced by the martyr, is "injustice collecting." Here the individual ruminates on all the raw deals and miscarriages of justice that he or she has endured. These might include the IRS audit, the boss's lack of appreciation, the rejected loan application. Injustice collectors don't recognize that life is rarely fair and that they alone have not been singled out for unjust treatment. Focusing on how they have been wronged (not on how they can change things for the better) only leaves them in a passive position from which they cannot easily escape.

Takeaway

When Everyday Masochists experience discomfort over pleasure they have "indulged in" or feel they have gotten more than they deserve, they often engage in "takeaway." In this torment, individuals deny themselves all or part of their pleasure by trying to undo it either directly or symbolically. Examples:

A hard-working employee takes a three-day weekend to go away with his family. Although no one expects it of him, he works until 9:00 P.M. the night before to make up for the time off.

After winning by a landslide, the newly elected student body president decides to skip her victory party. She tells herself she's just too tired to celebrate.

A man is offered a choice of exquisite fruits at a friend's home. He picks the one piece that is bruised.

Takeaway reflects the masochists' pleasure guilt. By denying themselves the full experience of pleasure, they are alleviating their feelings of wrongness and making peace with unacceptable desires.

Exercise: Torment Inventory

The Torment Inventory is primarily an awareness tool. It will test your motivation for change immediately because it requires both time and persistence. Yet the dividends it yields are high.

The inventory is first of all a behavioral record. It will show you precisely how and when you torment yourself. You can also use it to measure your progress against Everyday Masochism. Here's how it works.

Step 1: For the next fourteen days, record every torment you inflict on yourself. In a notebook turned on its side, transcribe on the left of the page (or pages) all the torments listed in this chapter. Divide the rest of the page(s) into seven columns, each signifying a day of the week—see the model on the next page. Every evening (preferably at the same hour) record whatever torments occurred that day, including the approximate time and the circumstances leading up to it.

Because most of us are unschooled in keeping this kind of diary, your early entries may be scarce or incomplete. As time

Torment	Mon	Tues	Wed	Thurs	Fri	Sat	Sun
Calamitizing							
Salting the Wound							
Screening							
Discounting							
Grouching							
Globalizing							
Word Processing							
Lamenting							
(Etc.)							

goes on and awareness develops, you will become more proficient at recognizing and remembering these flagellating experiences.

Step 2: In the third week, continue to record torments, but note which ones show up most often. Observe any patterns in when or where the torments occur. Notice also how you feel at the critical moment directly before you make yourself miserable.

Step 3: Put a check next to each torment you become aware of "in the act," as opposed to "after the fact." When most of your torments have checks next to them, go on to Step 4.

Step 4: You are now ready to start intervening in the torment process. Each time you notice it, stop yourself by shifting attention onto something else. If you are globalizing at work, for example, worrying about whether a minor error will cost you your job, shift your focus to another task that requires your attention or just mentally rearrange the furniture in your office. Usually this kind of cognitive diversion is enough to pull you out of the emotional quagmire although you may have to be tenacious in your refocusing.

Step 5: Sometimes, however, we obsessively lock into particular thoughts, and shifting attention is not so easy. If a torment is persistent, try the following: (1) Change your geography: walk around; go to another room; stand if you were sitting; sit if you were lying down. The physical change often provokes a cognitive shift. (2) Focus on sensation, observe your breathing, and deepen it. Notice which parts of your body feel tense. Breathe into those areas until they begin to relax. Put your attention on the soles of your feet for twenty seconds, now your ankles, calves, knees, and so on until you have worked your way up to your forehead. (3) Record the experience in your inventory; acknowledging the torment in writing can help diminish its control. (4) If circumstances allow, make a loud sound; vocal discharge often dissipates frustration and provides the shock value to break an obsessive chain of thoughts.

Step 6: Put an X next to each torment you have noticed and stopped in process. When most of your entries are so marked, move on to the next exercise.

Keep in mind the times you are likely to torment yourself—for example, in new situations when expectations are unclear or lying in bed before falling asleep. Familiarize yourself with your torment-prone times (they differ for everyone) and be particularly vigilant when they occur.

MUSTERBATIONS

This term, coined by psychologist Albert Ellis, describes another kind of tangle in which Everyday Masochists oppress themselves with a long list of rules they *must* live by. The rules are unbending, absolute, and always unreasonable, but they are seen as sacrosanct and cannot be challenged. Neo-Freudian Karen Horney called them the "tyranny of shoulds" because of their power to create suffering and emotional pain. When individuals fail to fulfill these imperatives, they feel guilty, disappointed in themselves, and often contemptuous of their failed efforts. One could even say there is a direct relationship between the amount of guilt a person feels and the number of shoulds he fails to meet.

The Everyday Masochist's inventory of "musts" and "shoulds" is long and trying: a young lawyer feels disappointed in herself for being less than pleasant with an obnoxious client; a teacher puts himself down for taking too much credit for his class's performance on a national achievement test; a mother feels guilty for getting sick before her daughter's birthday party. All these are examples of how EMs use "musterbation" to condemn their actions and create needless guilt.

The reality is that self-punishers not only feel guilty, they are overwhelmed by the sheer number of imperatives they have created for themselves. Daily living becomes an endless stream of obligations with very little room for the individual's own wants or preferences. Under such conditions, life loses its joy, and pleasure is overwhelmed by dictated demands.

No one can be considerate, patient, liked, or healthy all the time. Musterbations are the raw material from which self-imposed misery is made. But the pattern is so deeply ingrained that the individual hardly notices its omnipresence. When I pointed out his musterbatory behavior, one of my patients automatically responded, "I guess I shouldn't have so many shoulds!"

Exercise: Should Inventory

Step 1: Over a period of a week, take inventory of all your "shoulds" or "shouldn'ts." Give yourself time to reflect on exactly what these are. Consider how "shoulds" play a role in the following: sex, intimate relationships, friendships, work, family (particularly in relation to parents), leisure activity, and attitudes toward yourself. Record at least twenty, such as "I should never lose my temper," or "I should always be generous with my friends."

Step 2: Look over your inventory and determine if there are any patterns. If so, what do they suggest about you? Now consider which of your "shoulds" seem excessive or irrational? Which ones would be easiest to give up?

Step 3: Take a few at random and rewrite them, substituting the phrase "I want to" for "I should." What is the effect of this change? Are your statements now less or more accurate? What feelings do these new entries provoke? Rewrite the rest of your "shoulds" in the same way.

Step 4: Again take a few "shoulds" at random, but this time replace "I should" with "I don't have to." What is the effect of this change? Does it make sense? What feelings does it provoke? What can you learn from the change? Rewrite the rest of the entries in the same way. Are you ready to surrender any of your "shoulds"?

Chapter **Five**

Sadomasochist Tangos

No! Do come back with *all thy tortures!* . . .
Oh, come back, my unknown god!
My pain!
My last—happiness.

NIETZSCHE, *Thus Spake Zarathustra*

As the preceding chapter demonstrates, Everyday Masochists are their own worst enemies. Yet they often have help from others who are equally committed to abusing them. EMs attract and often seek out relationships with sadistic individuals who exploit and disrespect them. They engage in a dance of supremacy and submission, a sadomasochist tango, that is emotionally debilitating and psychologically destructive. In spite of their pain, they keep coming back for more.

WHAT IS A SADOMASOCHIST TANGO?

Immediately we think of a sexual scenario with ropes and studded leather bracelets. One person is cruel and punishing, the other takes pleasure in receiving pain. But as we noted

110

earlier, sadomasochism (S/M) extends beyond the boundaries of the sexual arena. A tango is any arrangement between
people that involves a chronic pattern of domination by one
individual over another, the imposition of suffering (mental
or physical) by that individual, and the collaboration and voluntary submission by the other person to this state of affairs.
Every tango is characterized by an inherent power imbalance.

Such dances exist not just in the personal realm, but also
between teacher and student, employer and employee, guru
and disciple, governments and governed, conqueror and con-
quered. They have existed since the beginning of human history and in virtually any situation where people interact.

Even in a society based on equality of rights and privileges,
power imbalances can be found everywhere. The family, perhaps the least democratic of all our institutions, is a model of
authoritarianism. The workplace, with its rigid hierarchy of
authority, spawns sadomasochistic interactions. Traditional
gender roles encourage men to dominate and control the
"weaker sex" as a natural right of their manhood. With such
influences on us, it is no wonder the tango is so commonplace. Equality is a hard ideal to attain.

The S/M relationships I have studied in my research have
one common characteristic. They repeat an earlier pattern
from at least one partner's family of origin. Those individuals
who come from homes in which their parents danced the
Sadomasochist Tango are more likely to take up the steps
themselves. The parental relationship provides the first vision
of how individuals interact. Psychologists believe this picture
is indelibly printed on the psyche and resurfaces unconsciously in the same way that a mother reacts to her child's
first illness as her own mother did. These imprints do not necessarily determine the future, but they have power over us if
we remain unaware of them and respond without mindful-
ness.

If a child was raised in an environment in which he or she

played the sadist or masochist in relation to the parents, that child is also more likely to fall into an S/M dynamic in adult relationships. Trained in submissive or dominating behavior by the family system, the individual gravitates back to a particular role because it is familiar and therefore easier to play. How often have we seen the family "victim" assume that position as an adult, or the childhood "bully" go on to browbeat spouse or co-workers.

Still, dancing the Sadomasochist Tango is not just a matter of parental modeling or early role training. With problems in standing up for themselves, saying "no," and wanting to be liked, Everyday Masochists are easy targets for the sadistic individual looking to tango. Once engaged in the dance, masochists hang in, hoping their goodwill, accumulated suffering, and infinite patience will win over their tormentors. Perhaps if they knew more about their dance partners, they would be less vulnerable.

PERSECUTOR PROFILES

Just as masochists are not lunatics who live for pain alone, neither are all sadists bloodthirsty relatives of Attila the Hun. Some are quite respectable citizens whose sadism is compartmentalized, expressed in only one or two areas of their lives. In many cases, people would be surprised to hear these individuals were capable of cruelty.

When we talk of sadism, we are really speaking of a continuum of behavior from the dyed-in-the-wool psychopath to the occasional victimizer. This comprises a great number of people, including the masochist who is quite capable of turning sadistic under the right circumstances.

Sadists seek out the vulnerable and the helpless with all the fervor of neophyte social workers on their first day at work.

But rather than show sympathy or concern, they are provoked by weakness; the more vulnerable the individual, the greater the contempt. Their intense reaction is to their own hidden feelings of fragility, which they cannot tolerate. Like so many people, they disdain in others what they hate in themselves.

Sadists do not respect their partner's sensibilities. They hit below the belt. If A harbors doubts about his masculinity, his sadistic intimate will poke at his uncertainty without a second thought. If B is unsure of her physical attractiveness, her abusive partner will use her doubts against her to gain the upper hand.

The sadist's primary interest is in the power, not the love, that relationships afford. Abusive individuals use sex, money, children, family—whatever is at their disposal—as weapons to gain control. They view a relationship as a battleground, a struggle for ascendancy and superiority.

In my research I asked individuals to describe sadistic characteristics of their partners. From these responses as well as from clinical observation, I have constructed six "persecutor profiles." These are the partners with whom Everyday Masochists commonly choose to tango.

Double-Dealers

Masters of deceit and fraud, double-dealers are individuals who manipulate another person's trust for their own advantage. Sometimes they are outrightly duplicitous; other times they merely lie through exclusion or misrepresentation. They often fail to keep their word, reveal confidences they have sworn to secrecy, and, in general, make promises they have little intention of keeping.

To such people, human relations are a game in which the only rule is to win. Honesty, integrity, and mutual respect are values that are foreign to them. In fact, they usually have covert contempt for those who espouse open, straightforward communication. They live by the code: Do it unto others before they do it unto you.

Unfortunately, double-dealers are difficult to spot. They have learned to present themselves as people of high virtue, and it takes a certain amount of shared history to catch them in a lie. Even then, they may appear absolutely ingenuous or profoundly contrite. They are Machiavellian in their intrigues and are unwilling to consider the destructiveness of their actions. Even when their dishonesty has caused the demise of a relationship, they may deny their responsibility.

Double-dealers frequently choose martyrs as dance partners because the latter's brooding passivity allows them room to weave their web of deceit.

Adversaries

Put these people in the most cooperative of settings and they will find a way to inject competition into it. Every experience is seen as a contest in which they feel compelled to come out on top. They must be the smartest or the shrewdest or the most attractive, even the healthiest. Those who challenge them are considered enemies and treated accordingly. In formal, competitive settings, their behavior is passable and may even serve them well. But in all other circumstances, particularly in the realms of love and sexuality, their actions are out of place and experienced by others as brutish and insensitive.

Living with such individuals is treacherous. One-upmanship is their chosen sport, but one-up means that someone is one-down, and that someone is usually the intimate partner. Since adversaries feel genuine contempt for losers and second stringers, the result is a continuing cycle of deprecation followed by disdain.

Adversaries are fond of pointing out how their attitude, idea, or possession is better than anyone's else's. They are skilled at finding the flaw in another individual's argument in order to demonstrate the superiority of their own. At best, they react with lukewarm interest to their partner's successes. And if those successes overshadow their own, they will be outrightly hostile and critical.

These individuals have a security problem. They feel deeply inadequate and a continual show of their predominance is necessary to neutralize their self-doubt. Unlike perfectionists, who are trying to prove their worth through strangulating self-improvement, adversaries climb on the backs of others, pushing them down in order to gain ascendancy. They are people who cannot tolerate second best, and their victims are simply those whose backs are available for their use.

One-upmanship is also a way of maintaining control. The ascendant position allows an individual to captain the relationship, determining such things as how money is spent, who the couple's friends will be, child-rearing practices, and even the degree of shared intimacy. Individuals who are afraid they will be overwhelmed or trapped if they allow others to have some control fall into this group.

Adversaries are attracted to perfectionists. Their need to be "top dog" meshes nicely with the perfectionist's constant denigration of his own performance.

Exploiters

These are individuals who use people as objects for their own gain. They see the world revolving around them and existing for their pleasure alone. Others are thought of as mere audiences to witness and appreciate their talents. Such individuals have an exaggerated view of their own importance and feel entitled to special treatment. They judge any occurrence solely on the basis of whether it is good for them; their empathy for others can be dispensed in an eye dropper. They seem to have no ability to understand or appreciate the other person's point of view: If it is at odds with theirs, it is summarily dismissed.

Exploiters use people and discard them when they are no longer of value. Their list of former friends is always extensive, and they often pursue relationships purely to gain advantage. They are opportunistic and maintain a solipsistic view of events. Ironically, they are not really interested in causing their partner pain. This occurs inadvertently as a function of their disregard and lack of interest. Their narcissistic attitude is cruel and hurtful because it does not acknowledge the other person's experience, feelings, or needs. Living with an exploiter is as lonely an experience as it is painful.

Exploiters typically seek out pleasers because the latter make good audiences (they are "naturally" supportive) and will allow themselves to be used if they feel it will earn them love.

Invalidators

These are the most insidious of sadists because their actions are subtle enough to keep their victims unaware or uncertain of their motives. If confronted, they frequently claim to be misunderstood; they'll claim that their intentions were not to disparage, but to state a fact or merely point out a flaw in order to give their partners an opportunity to improve themselves. How thoughtful of them. Most people would prefer they kept their brand of altruism to themselves.

The truth about invalidators is that they are habitués of the game: "I'm okay, you're not." That is their constant message, which, if delivered often enough, amounts to cruel and unusual punishment. They are masters of these tricks: disdain or disgust, expressed not with words but in a fleeting facial expression; long and awkward silences in response to requests for support or encouragement; a condescending tone in the voice expressing the sentiment, "It's an effort but I suppose I can put up with you"; "helpful" reminders of past failures delivered at the beginning of a new undertaking; direct statements of doubt and skepticism; devaluation of another's opinions or feelings.

Invalidators behave with disdain toward any acts of pride or assertion by their partners. Like adversaries, they cannot tolerate other people's success and respond by voiding or negating the accomplishment. They may show how another's achievement is of little consequence, point out a bigger challenge that has yet to be met, or insist that luck or circumstance played a key role. Anything to nullify the triumph and undermine the partner.

The motives of these individuals are complex. Some are operating out of anger, expressing their feelings by tearing down the object of their rage. Others are disappointed in their partners and are punishing them for not meeting expectations. Still others are projecting their own feelings of unworth. They "disown" what they feel inside themselves by seeing it in someone else.

Invalidators like to dance with avoiders and pleasers. Avoiders fail to notice their constant subversion; pleasers are stimulated to try harder by the promise of love suggested in the invalidator's devaluations (If you were just a little smarter, prettier . . .).

Faultfinders

So called because they indulge in belittling, ridiculing, and criticizing their partners' weaknesses like drill sergeants with a bunch of green recruits. The faultfinder's game is simple: make someone else appear wrong in order to establish and maintain supremacy in the relationship. As with so many sadists, aggressing on others takes the focus off their own inadequacies. "It's your fault" means "I am blameless." "You're a fool" implies "I am not."

Faultfinders use a variety of indignities to get their point across including:

> *Insult:* "I can't talk to you about my work because you don't have the brains to follow me!"
> *Taunt:* "What kind of man are you? A worm has more guts!"
> *Reproach:* "You should know better than to want sex at a time like this!"
> *Blame:* "You've always held me back from being more successful than I could be!"

Many faultfinders also use their intimate relationships to displace frustration. If they had a bad day at work, they take it out on the kids. If they are caught in traffic, they lay their irritation on their spouses. The other person is simply the target on which to discharge the accumulated negative emotion. Never mind what the target experiences. Faultfinders either ignore the impact of their criticism or rationalize their actions as helpful to the recipient: "He needs to learn how to take criticism." Some go so far as to view ridicule as a legitimate form of motivating behavior. They fail to take into account the harm that a steady diet of put-downs and insults can have on their partners' self-esteem.

Like any repetitive behavior, the faultfinder's taunts and reproaches soon become a habit. Even if the original domination or displacement needs are no longer active, the pattern may continue as a style of interaction. Like the proverbial wife joke, it may not have malicious intent but its effects are still experienced as demeaning.

Faultfinders prefer avoiders as partners because these Everyday Masochists, with their tendency to hide their heads in the sand, are usually oblivious to the sadist's real motives and will tolerate a great deal of abuse. Avoiders commonly excuse their partner's constant criticism by viewing it as something wholly different than it is. (She's just letting off steam!)

Tyrants

Tyrants are the heavyweights on the list. They maintain absolute dominance in their relationships by threatening, intimidating, and menacing their victims. They strut ominously, browbeat, bully, and terrorize. They are particularly adept at spotting people's most hidden sensitivity and using it to subjugate them when the time is right. They are not adverse to raking someone over the coals or humiliating them in public. They may tell cruel jokes. They use fear to manipulate, and physical abuse is not beneath them.

In the course of an argument, their favorite tactic is to stand at an intrusive distance from their antagonist and speak loudly. If they are verbally adroit, they will use the cutting power of their sharp tongues to slice up their opposition. If they are physically large, they will intimidate with their size. They can be very persistent and insistent, wearing down their partner with the sheer energy of their harassment. And they give the impression (true or not) that they are capable of doing anything to get what they want. The "macho" and "bitch" stereotypes fit into this category.

These are generally angry people who have been abused and humiliated themselves in an earlier time and are now engaging in a reversal of roles. "Once the oppressed, now the oppressor" goes an old folk saying that aptly describes their turnaround. Tyrants cannot tolerate giving power to others because their childhood experience has taught them that they will be squelched into submission. Their debasement has provoked a Nietzschean view of things. They see only two kinds of people in the world: master and slave. And after a demeaning start, they have no doubt in which group they belong.

Power overshadows all aspects of their lives. Sex is an area where pleasure takes a backseat to dominance. Relationships are territorial arrangements defined by a struggle for control. Love is a four-letter word never really comprehended. And work is a daily dogfight for supremacy.

Tyrants have rigid minds that tend to see things as black or white. Someone is either a friend or an enemy, a supporter or a detractor. Right and wrong is a clearcut matter with no exceptions or qualifications. The tyrant is always right; it's that simple—although living with the tyrant is anything but.

These sadists don't discriminate in their selection of masochistic partners. They will dance with anyone who is intimidated by their browbeating. Since EMs have trouble standing up for themselves, any of the four types is susceptible to the tyrant's abuse.

ARE YOU IN A SADOMASOCHISTIC RELATIONSHIP?

In spite of our ability to recognize S/M dynamics in the relationships of friends and family, we often miss the clues in our own lives. Particularly when our relationships are not full-blown tangos but contain only a few elements, we tend to overlook them as aberrations or regard them as the price everyone pays for intimacy.

Are you in a Sadomasochist Tango? The short quiz below will help you find out. Answer yes or no to each of the following questions (a tango test specifically designed for the workplace appears in Chapter 6):

1. My partner is critical of me in front of others.
2. I often feel less competent than my partner.
3. My partner demeans my efforts or opinions.
4. When we get into an argument, I don't feel I can stand up to my partner.
5. My partner is more interested in getting his or her needs met than in my welfare.
6. To avoid a fight I usually overlook my partner's abuse.
7. I can't trust my partner to keep his or her word.
8. My partner gets satisfaction in putting me down.
9. When it comes to important matters, I give my partner's opinion more weight than my own.
10. My partner has to be in control.
11. If I stand up to my partner, I'm afraid he or she will be provoked.
12. My partner takes unnecessary advantage of me.
13. My partner has to have the last word.
14. I don't feel my partner supports my feelings.
15. My partner picks on my errors and mistakes.

If you answered "yes" on four to seven of these items, your relationship requires some help. A talk with your partner about the sadomasochistic characteristics in your interaction would be helpful. Seven to ten "yeses", and you should seek professional intervention. Consider couple counseling. Above ten, your relationship is in the danger zone. Reconsider your commitment.

THE TANGOS

Over the years I have worked with many couples who dance the Sadomasochist Tango. The therapy is always initiated by the partner whose toes are stepped on, but generally neither dancer is aware of the S/M dynamics in the relationship.

These dances are insidious. They can whirl you around the dance floor without your formal consent, and they can sneak up on you after years of marriage.

Tango 1: Now You See Him, Now You Don't

TYPICAL DANCERS: Exploiters and pleasers.

THE DANCE: Kevin and Joyce, both previously married, have been dating for the past two years. Joyce wants a committed relationship; Kevin is uncertain. The tension surrounding this issue is always present in their interactions. Kevin's pattern is to profess great interest and affection. He will call every day, send flowers, run errands, and be attentive and caring. Then, without apparent reason, he will withdraw, fail to keep dates, and drop from sight.

In response, Joyce automatically assumes she has done something to alienate him: Perhaps she has been too demanding or inattentive; maybe she hasn't been making enough of an effort to keep him interested. She's confused by his actions and searches her memory for anything that might offer a clue. When nothing comes to mind, she makes excuses for him. He needs a little breathing room, or he's probably working too hard and doesn't feel he would be good company.

As Joyce tries to come to grips with Kevin's inconsistent involvement, he resurfaces and begins to show renewed interest. He is once again his helpful, charming, and seductive self. He either acts as if he hasn't withdrawn, or he minimizes his disappearance with excuses: "I was preoccupied with a new project at work"; "I've been very busy remodeling my kitchen"; and so forth. Joyce is so happy to have him back that she accepts his lame alibis.

She allows herself to become involved again. But just as she begins to forget the past, he starts the dance once more. He misses a dinner date, then blames her for the slipup. He shows up hours late for a party. He stops calling or returning her calls. In emotional pain, Joyce swears she'll never see him again. Several weeks later the affable and charming Kevin reappears. This time he is twice as sweet and considerate. He apologizes for his thoughtlessness and promises he will never leave her again. He's had time to think it over, and he's ready to make it work.

Despite the fact that his behavior has provoked deep feelings of self-doubt and caused her no small amount of emotional trauma, Joyce accepts him back, hoping that this time things will be different. "I just can't live without him," she tells herself.

THE DANCE STEPS: He is seductive; she is seduced; he withdraws, she blames herself and makes excuses for him; he is seductive; she takes him back; repeat.

ANALYSIS: Kevin is not really interested in the relationship, only in the seduction. He gets satisfaction from the challenge of getting someone to dance with him. Once he has done that, he has little use for the partner and withdraws. After a while he resumes the seduction again. His lack of concern for the effect of his behavior on Joyce reveals an exploiter profile. Underneath, he is fearful of intimacy and unwilling to risk commitment. He expresses his fears by running hot and cold.

Joyce plays a classic pleaser role. She blames the situation on herself and makes excuses for her lover. She closes her eyes to the possibility she is being exploited. She has, of course, the option to stop dancing, but she never exercises it. Instead, she stays on hoping Kevin will change or see the light even when the constant repetition of the pattern should have warned her otherwise.

Like all Everyday Masochists, Joyce tolerates an intolerable situation because she feels inadequate and afraid that her partner's actions are really a reflection of her undesirability. She is willing to take the bad to get the good even when the price is her own self-esteem. She believes she's acting out of love, but what kind of love is she getting in return? In reality, she's afraid to cut him loose and start over again with someone else.

Tango 2: Hitting Below the Belt

TYPICAL DANCERS: Faultfinders and avoiders.

THE DANCE: In their late forties, Rachel and Sid are a modern version of the proverbial "Jack Sprat and wife." They are as different as night and day: He's a quiet, passive person; she's an outgoing social dynamo. He's thrifty; she likes to spend money. He believes in rules and discipline for the children; she advocates giving them the freedom to make their own choices. Psychologists would call theirs a complementary relationship. It is their differences that attracted them to each other in the first place and their differences that are their undoing.

As the years have gone by, Rachel has become increasingly intolerant of her husband's nature. She has slipped into a pattern of continually picking at Sid, denigrating his opinions and ridiculing his behavior. For example, when Sid offers an opinion, her response is something like: "You don't know what you're talking about big shot. You're always wrong." When he fixes the plumbing, she taunts: "Well, I hope this will be better than the last job you did." When he gets a promotion, she responds: "It's about time, but I wonder how you pulled the wool over their eyes."

Sid's reaction to the continuing harangue of put-downs is to placate his wife. His voice softens. He tries to change the subject. He offers to do things for her. His sweetness only stimulates her derision. Her verbal jabbing becomes more personal and cuts deeper. Now she really lets him have it: "My mother told me not to marry you in the first place";

"You're getting to be shaped like a pear. I'm embarrassed to be seen with you."

These remarks have their affect. He shrinks further into himself, goes into the kitchen and eats a box of cookies or sits in front of the television the rest of the day. What he doesn't do is fight back. He doesn't feel strong enough to counter her aggression. He withdraws, hoping to wait her out. But rather than gain her good graces, his passivity encourages her cruelty. She hits him below the belt, dragging his secret vulnerabilities out of the closet and trampling them with sneers and sarcasm.

THE DANCE STEPS: She is critical, he is placating; she is cruel, he withdraws; she escalates, he withdraws; repeat.

ANALYSIS: Rachel, who is profoundly disappointed in her own life and angry at her husband for any number of past sins, expresses these feelings in a daily barrage of ridicule and humiliation. Although she would be further angered if Sid stood up to her, his weakness stimulates her contempt and gives her carte blanche to displace any and all frustrations onto a convenient target. Clearly she is a faultfinder who uses her husband as a whipping boy to hide from her own problems. Since all their difficulties are his fault, she doesn't have to take responsibility for her own contributions.

Like all avoiders, Sid hopes that if he sits them out Rachel's outbursts will go away. He is intimidated by her anger and feels unable to stand up to it. To survive he has learned to tune out her sharp tongue and wait for the danger to pass. But his placating demeanor provokes contempt and earns him more derision.

Sid is afraid of his own feelings of rage. Inside he feels the hurt and anger that his wife's constant beratings have caused. Yet he is afraid that if he vents these feelings, even minimally, they will become uncontrollable and overwhelm him. He would rather swallow the bitter pill she hands out.

His actions are not wholly strategic. He believes Rachel is at least partly right about him: He is a failure and perhaps a coward. She is right to be disappointed because, if the truth be told, he is disappointed in himself. He cannot stand up to his wife's abuse because he feels a sense of powerlessness. Given his own doubts, he does not even recognize the cruelty in her taunts. On some deeper level, he believes his suffering is deserved.

Tango 3: The Check Is in the Mail and Other Deceits

TYPICAL DANCERS: Double-Dealers and martyrs.

THE DANCE: When Sally met Darrell on a Caribbean cruise, she could hardly believe he was real. There was no doubt in her mind that he was the man she had been looking for: He was handsome, urbane, successful, and sensitive. After sitting next to him at dinner that first night, she was even more convinced. His values, his opinions, and his understanding of human relationships were compatible with her own. He was perfect and she felt herself slipping into infatuation.

Darrell said he was looking for a strong woman who was assertive and knew what she wanted. Traditional women bored him; they were too predictable. He was emphatic that he wanted a sensual partner who liked nothing better than to spend the afternoon exchanging lazy caresses. He was tired of one-night stands and singles' bars and craved a monogamous relationship that was built on deep affection and loyalty. He insisted that the love relationship in his life be central and paramount, that it should be like "a well from which all emotional sustenance is drawn". All these declarations filled Sally with utter delight. Here, finally, was her ideal man.

The rest of the cruise was as exciting as the first days, and they looked forward to continuing their relationship when they returned home. The lived in neighboring cities, a short plane ride away. They pledged to make their weekends together as exciting and wonderful as their lovely Caribbean days had been.

But things began to change quickly when they got home, particularly in their sexual relationship. Darrell didn't seem interested. He never initiated their love-making and wasn't a thoughtful or giving partner. He was quick and fierce, not at all the caring, sultry lover he had been earlier. Then, too, he seemed to be put off when Sally asked for more time in bed together.

As the weeks passed, their lovemaking became briefer and more infrequent. Sally would fly up only to find that Darrell had made plans with friends for the whole weekend, leaving the two of them barely a moment to be alone. In the evening, he would drink too much and fall asleep before they ever made it to the bedroom.

When, with great difficulty, she told him of her disappointment, he reacted indignantly and insisted she was the one who was aloof and disinterested. The strength of his conviction confused her. Could she be mistaken?

Sally found herself sitting at home alone angrily recounting the events of their relationship. She hated going out to dinner with Darrell. When she tried to order for herself, he would cut her off and tell the waiter what she would have. She bitterly recalled his words on the cruise about "a strong woman who was assertive and knew what she wanted."

As time went on her confusion increased. There were obvious signs that he had other women in his life, although he fervently denied it. Yet even more alarming was the fact that the important, supportive relationship he had ballyhooed did not exist. Sally felt he treated her more like a date than an equal partner. She had revealed her own feelings of inadequacy, vulnerability, and fear to him. He was closemouthed, never talking about himself in a personal way. She didn't feel close to him and wasn't sure if it was her or him.

Her confusion turned to acrimony. She felt victimized and sorry for herself. She started keeping a mental record of his deceits and all other ways he had wronged her. But rather than talk to him about it, she kept it all to herself. She became brooding and resentful. When she was with him she would sulk and pout. Her anger leaked out in oppositional behavior. If he liked a particular movie, she had five good reasons why it wasn't any good. She was taciturn when he was happy, tired when he was full of energy.

Despite her show of feeling miserable, Darrell acted as if nothing was wrong. Three months later, without any warning, he ended the relationship.

THE DANCE STEPS: He misrepresents himself; she believes him; he is revealed, she broods; he continues to deceive, she is passively aggressive.

ANALYSIS: Double-dealers like Darrell manipulate their partners by insisting that what is false is true and what is true is false. Their strategy is simply to repeat a lie often and resolutely enough so that it will be believed. Consequently, they are always denying their past statements or actions, blaming conflicts on miscommunication, and pleading earnestly that they have been misunderstood. They manipulate with their charm and sincerity. The effect of their subterfuge is to create confusion and bewilderment, which serves as a smokescreen for their falsehoods.

Sally's righteous indignation, brooding moods, and stubborn oppositionist stance identify her as a typical martyr. Even her spiteful attempts to make Darrell miserable hurt her more than him. By not confronting her lover or deciding to write him off, she surrendered her power and allowed herself to be mistreated longer than she had to.

Tango 4: Pulling the Rug Out From Under

TYPICAL DANCERS: Invalidators and avoiders.

THE DANCE: Laura and Russell, with two children and twenty years of marriage behind them, thought they had the perfect relationship. They built their life around home and family loyalty. They shared common values and a similar moderate temperament. They rarely argued and were quick to make up when they did. In general, they were considerate and respectful of each other.

As Laura reached her middle forties and her children moved out of the house, she felt a deep sense of boredom; her life was going nowhere. She began thinking about returning to school and reclaiming the career in law that she had given up to raise a family. She knew it was the right thing for her, but she was concerned about her husband's reaction.

Russell was a tolerant man and familiar enough with American life in the eighties to know that his wife's new plans were not atypical. But he was also very comfortable in his life-style. He enjoyed the role of breadwinner and father. About personal matters, he was a traditionalist. Still, when they discussed Laura's return to law school, he understood her feelings and went along with her wishes.

But after six months of Laura in the library every night he began to feel abandoned. With the kids no longer around, he was forced to make his own meals and eat by himself. He was lonely and felt neglected and forgotten. Yet, having agreed to his wife's plan, he felt he could not renege on the deal.

Without realizing it, his growing opposition began to take expression in the form of subtle undermining. At first he refused to talk with her about her experiences at school. Then he began to make disparaging comments about the law profession. He showed no interest in her achievements although she was getting good grades, and when she was obviously under stress during exam time, he was particularly demanding. When she came home excited with the news that she had made Law Review, he changed the subject almost immediately. And on at least two occasions he arranged business dinners that required her participation on the night before an important test.

At every turn he was unsupportive. He made demeaning remarks about her inability to understand the finer points of law. He seemed to enjoy dwelling on her mistakes and was fond of telling her she wasn't tough enough to make it in the profession. His favorite phrase was "the law is an ass and all lawyers are assh---s." He refused to participate in any social activities run by the school. He showed a marked disinterest in her new friends. Once he came home with tickets to Paris that conflicted with important school activities. When she begged him to change the dates, he retorted, "It's now or never." He even tightened the purse strings, making it difficult for her to pay for books and other school necessities.

To all this Laura looked the other way. She could feel his unhappiness with her new career, but she downplayed the extent of his sabotage. She refused to believe that Russell would behave that way. She rationalized his actions by assuming he was having difficulties at work and that he missed his children, who were rarely around. Even when his remarks were obviously demeaning and hurtful, she never acknowledged their cruel intent. And although his lack of support caused her to doubt herself, she pretended he was only joking or simply letting off steam. She felt so guilty about the time she spent away from home that she didn't dare confront him. She was sure he would accuse her of being a bad wife or a selfish opportunist, two things she was afraid were true. Like every avoider, she put off dealing with the situation by telling herself things would work out sooner or later.

The dance came to a climax when Russell refused to go to her graduation. Laura was stunned by his pronouncement and she broke down into prolonged sobbing. At the end of the outburst, she had a sudden burst of clarity. The past three years of Russell's undermining, invalidating behavior were clear to her for the first time. Yet she felt it was too late. The situation was hopeless. Without responding to his refusal, she went to her graduation alone.

THE DANCE STEPS: He undermines her, she fails to notice; he escalates, she avoids; repeat.

ANALYSIS: Invalidation is an insidious form of sadistic response because the motivation behind it can be so easily misread. Is one's spouse undermining or genuinely uninterested? Is he an ally or an enemy? As a repeated pattern of interaction, invalidation can be as devastating as any other form of psychic cruelty because it pulls the rug out from under a person without warning. Other forms of sadistic behavior are easier to recognize and defend against. We look to our intimate partners for support and acceptance. Every lasting relationship is built on positive regard, trust, and goodwill. Invalidation undermines that foundation and provokes self-doubt, sometimes under the guise of good intentions.

Russell's invalidating behavior did not stem from cruelty or a desire to hurt his wife. He loved her and did not want to lose her. But his anger at her changing their relationship after so many years drove him to obstruct her new career and diminish her in the process.

Laura colluded with his sabotage by shutting her eyes to what was happening. Her own guilt about leaving the home kept her from acknowledging his invalidation and drawing limits on it. It never occurred to her that Russell's actions were hostile or that he might have an ax to grind. She wanted to pretend that everything was fine between them. Her inattention only gave him more room to undermine her.

Tango 5: Let's Get Physical

TYPICAL DANCERS: Tyrants and all EM styles.

THE DANCERS: Life was not going well for the Claytons. Peter, an architect by training, had lost his job, and his wife's nursing salary just about kept them afloat. After Peter's mother died of cancer, he went through a serious bout of depression that lasted the better part of a year. When he started looking for work again, he began drinking heavily.

It was during this period that he started physically abusing Andrea, his wife. At first he only verbalized his frustrations. He blew the smallest incidents out of proportion and blamed her for all their problems: she was the one who had suggested living in a place where there were no jobs; she was spending too much money; she was putting too much pressure on him. Then, after drinking heavily, he started to push and shove her around, all the while cursing and belittling her. Finally, he escalated to hitting her.

Andrea was petrified. She had never seen him so ugly or cruel. She had not thought it possible that the man who had promised five years earlier to love and cherish her could behave in such a brutish and obscene manner. She was afraid of being hurt, afraid for their relationship, and afraid of the shame that his actions brought on both of them. She was living a nightmare, and each day she awoke with a knot in her stomach.

To assuage him, she stayed out of his way. Whenever he was drinking, she made herself scarce. She became submissive in order not to provoke him. She avoided conflict at all costs, even making up stories to mollify him. Once, when she got into a minor car accident, she found herself shaking violently and then bursting into hysterical tears. It was not the accident that shook her up but the thought of telling her husband.

She hid it all from family and friends. She was so deeply

ashamed that she told no one. Peter's behavior was not just a reflection on him, she told herself. She had chosen to make a life with him. What happened between them was as much her responsibility as his. And it was not really his fault. They had gone through a terrible period, and he was just reacting to all the frustrations. True, his behavior was terrible. But you couldn't really blame the man; it was the alcohol talking. Underneath, Peter was decent and caring. Her only choice was to wait it out. When he got a job, everything would work out.

But things did not get better. Peter's drinking continued, the physical violence continued, and Andrea was barely able to function. She felt hopeless and paralyzed. Her friends began to notice the change in her. They wondered about the black-and-blue marks but didn't want to embarrass her with questions. One day her sister took her aside and gently probed for some answers. Andrea broke down and told her the whole story. Her sister insisted she call the police but Andrea wouldn't hear of it. She settled reluctantly on couple counseling as the least frightening of her alternatives. The night before talking to Peter about it, she couldn't sleep. She was deathly afraid of his reaction. Fortunately, he was so miserable himself that he consented to her request without incident. A long period of substance abuse therapy and couple counseling followed.

THE DANCE STEPS: He is verbally abusive, she is submissive; he escalates to physical abuse, she avoids confrontation; he continues, she is paralyzed by fear and shame.

ANALYSIS: Here is the Sadomasochist Tango in its extreme; an abusive partner and a submissive one caught in a fierce dance in which the latter is emotionally and physically mistreated.

Peter displaced his anger and frustrations onto Andrea, and her pained reaction was of little consequence to him. His mother's death and his failure to find work created great strain, but it was alcohol that put him over the edge. Andrea became the scapegoat for his self-hatred and misery. Rather than face himself, he struck out at the most accessible target. Curiously, Andrea felt responsible for his behavior, and this distortion coupled with her fear and shame kept her from taking action to stop him.

Andrea chose a passive response by becoming more compliant and shrinking as far into the woodwork as possible. Her actions merely gave Peter greater room for mistreatment. Submissiveness in no way deterred him; in fact, it fed his contempt.

By not setting limits on his abuse at the outset, Andrea abdicated her influence in the relationship. Peter's behavior was intolerable, and it was important for her to tell him so before he escalated into physical violence. Once that happened, she lost sight of her options: seeking outside help; leaving the relationship; or pursuing legal remedies. In not taking the appropriate and necessary strong actions, she jeopardized her own health and well-being.

It is just this kind of strong stand that Everyday Masochists fear making. They are deeply ashamed of their situation and assume they have neither the grounds nor the strength to support forceful actions. Their failure to respond decisively only makes things worse. Andrea's responsibility was not in creating Peter's abuse, but in tolerating it for as long as she did.

Tango 6: Partners in Criticism

TYPICAL DANCERS: Adversaries and perfectionists.

THE DANCERS: Lee is a twenty-seven-year-old chemist who works for a nationally known pharmaceutical company. He is a valued employee, hard working, responsible, and professional. In the lab, he is a model of efficiency and exactitude. His personal life is governed much the same way. He is fastidious, cautious, and predictable. He follows the same routines day after day. His world is governed by rules and procedures. Nothing is left to chance.

Despite the fact that Lee has been singled out by management as a top prospect for high-level promotion, his own feelings do not reflect his employer's confidence. He worries about making mistakes and getting called on the carpet. His annual evaluation always produces a week of sleepless nights. Speaking before a group causes him undue anxiety. He experiences any criticism of his performance as demeaning. In short, he is a man who is sensitive to failure and very hard on himself.

Alexis, Lee's girlfriend, also in her twenties, is a hard-driving associate editor for a popular women's magazine. She is competitive, passionate, and ambitious. Attracted to Lee by his reliable and stable nature, she is nonetheless critical of his caution and predictability. Both are rising stars in their respective corporate worlds, but their personal styles are dramatically different.

In fact, much of how Lee does things is galling to Alexis. Not valuing meticulousness, she doesn't understand how it can possibly pay off. Her strength lies in her ability to see the big picture, the larger trends—to know what issues are important to women today and tomorrow. Details are distractions to her.

Alexis's habit of jumping on Lee's point of view and demonstrating the superiority of her own perspective is a familiar pattern, known even to their friends. That Lee maintains impossible standards for himself and is obsessive about minor flaws further aggravates the situation. At times it appears they are fighting over who can criticize him more. Here are two typical conversations:

ALEXIS: Do you ever stop being a scientist?
LEE: What?

ALEXIS: You make love according to the scientific method.

LEE: What does that mean?

ALEXIS: You punch in, proceed from step one through step seven, tidy up any mess, then punch out. Never any variation.

LEE: What do you suggest?

ALEXIS: Let yourself go like I do.

LEE: Okay, I'll try harder.

ALEXIS: Why don't you try softer?

*   *   *

LEE: I'm screwing up at work again. I'm three weeks behind on this new project.

ALEXIS: The new tranquilizer? Don't worry about it, they're used to your delays by now.

LEE: Yeah, but this is a big project.

ALEXIS: You know why you're always behind? Because you spend too much time checking and rechecking details. For God's sake, stop acting like a Swiss watchmaker.

LEE: But if I'm not careful . . .

ALEXIS: (interrupts) You're a real jerk, you know that. They've already got you working till eight at night five days a week. You don't see me getting trapped like that.

LEE: But that's what they demand. I swear, if I listened to you I'd lose my job.

ALEXIS: Bull. They're not going to fire you. Listen to me. I never have any of this kind of trouble.

THE DANCE STEPS: He is self-critical; she joins in; he is defensive, she is superior; repeat.

ANALYSIS: Alexis is plainly contemptuous of Lee. We might wonder why she even continues in a relationship with him until we consider her sadistic style. She is an adversary, hooked into the competition. Her game is to prove she is better than him, to put herself one up whenever possible. Hence her quickness to jump on his admissions of failure and show her superiority: "I never have any of this kind of trouble. . . ."

We learned earlier how the victorious timber wolf will instinctively spare the life of his adversary in reaction to an expression of helplessness. Human opponents are less predictable. Some react with assurance and support to expressions of helplessness and self-abnegation. Others, like Alexis, are actually spurred on by disclosures of weakness. Their contempt is evoked by admissions of vulnerability and they feel compelled to kick the victim when he is down.

Lee is a perfectionist whose self-criticism plays directly into Alexis's need for predominance. They are a perfect fit in their alliance to demean his character.

But why would Lee choose a partner like Alexis? Surely he must feel pained by her deprecating remarks and one-upmanship. Why didn't he find a lover who could give him assurance and affirmation? The answer is contained in the perfectionist's distorted thinking. To Lee, anyone who offers support instead of stress is not to be trusted. The critic keeps him on his toes, driving him closer to perfection while the cheerleader offers indiscriminate support that is not worth anything in the long run.

The self-defeating nature of Lee's choice also suggests that he picked Alexis because she affirmed his flawed vision of himself. Never mind that her judgments were self-interested or biased by a neurotic need for predominance. In choosing her, his inadequacy and self-contempt triumphed. He recreated the same dynamic with her that he had with his critical, dissatisfied parents.

Hapless Victim or Co-Instigator?

In observing the dynamics of the Sadomasochist Tango, it is often hard to see beyond the abuses of the sadist to the role of the Everyday Masochist. EMs are not just innocent by-standers who have failed to set limits or stop the destructive dance; they are individuals who set themselves up to be victimized by continually choosing the wrong partners. Letty, an attorney with a flair for courtroom work, was as frustrated by her personal relationships as she was successful in her career. What was the problem? She continually pursued men who were as successful as she but who put their work ahead of their personal lives. Always traveling, working late, or fighting a deadline, they would become increasingly unavailable as the months went by, leaving her alone to wonder where she went wrong.

Her friend Karen, also an attorney, had a similar problem, but she chose a different sort of man: the aloof macho type who abused her psychologically and could not meet her emotional needs for warmth and support. She moved through one relationship after another without recognizing that each dancer was interchangeable with the last.

Both women selected men who could not give them what they wanted. Still, they persisted in repeating their mistakes despite the hurt, anger, and frustration they felt each time. Although they might appear as hapless pawns to the outsider, neither was an innocent victim of their partner's actions.

REFUSING TO DANCE

Here are some general rules that will help the Everyday Masochist avoid getting ensnared in yet another destructive tango.

1. *Begin your intimate relationships slowly.* Don't allow romantic illusions to sweep you away. Listen to your intuition and your good common sense. Strong physical attraction is not enough. The perfect date may make a lousy life partner. Remember that early in a

relationship both individuals usually present themselves as the person they'd like to be, not the person they are. Look beyond the facade. Acknowledge what you really need in a partner and ask yourself whether this individual is capable and willing to give it to you.

2. *Know who the predators are.* Watch for danger signs: small deceits; self-absorption; condescension; hostile treatment of others. How does this individual use power? How does he relate to those who are vulnerable? Is she capable of softening and responding from her heart? Does he fit any of the six persecutor profiles?

3. *Get out of the rescue game.* By now you know that saving souls is best left to missionaries. Rescuers inevitably get bored or burned and rarely get their needs met.

4. *Intervene early in sadomasochistic patterns.* It is harder to stop dancing a Sadomasochist Tango once you've been doing it for a while. Sweeping your misgivings under the rug or making excuses for your partner are usually signs you don't want to face the situation. Remember, it's only going to get worse, not better.

5. *Give yourself the basic right.* In relationships, there is one fundamental prerogative that each partner can claim: to say how you want and don't want to be treated. Everyday Masochists "forget" to assert this right and their sadistic partners have a stake in not reminding them.

6. *Regularly discuss your relationship with your partner.* Abuses are less likely to occur when communication is frequent. Below are some suggestions to keep in mind at these "state of the union" meetings.

"Don'ts"

- Don't blame. Use statements that begin with "I" rather than "you." Blaming generates a defensive, not a receptive response.

- Don't put yourself down. Sadists will use your self-criticism against you. They do not respect humility.
- Don't weaken your words with overqualification or indirectness. These will be interpreted as signs of weakness.
- Don't sabotage the power of your statements with inappropriate smiling, seductive body language, or other actions that indicate you're not serious.
- Don't let fears of disapproval and abandonment govern your actions. Disapproval is a small price to pay for ending a tango, and fears of abandonment are usually exaggerated and overdrawn.
- Don't get discouraged. You may have to fight for the right to be treated with respect, but it is a struggle worth undertaking.

"Dos"

- Be clear about your feelings (the anger as well as the hurt).
- Be direct, firm, and persistent in your communication.
- State your limits. Which of your partner's behaviors feel like "hitting below the belt?" Let it be known that some actions are intolerable and unacceptable to you.
- Communicate the message that tearing down your self-esteem is not good for you and in the long run is destructive to the relationship.

7. *Consider getting professional help.* If talking doesn't work or escalates the tango, you may need third-party assistance. An experienced couple therapist can provide a safe environment in which to express feelings and can help mediate and solve problems.
8. *Know when to get out.* Don't be afraid to think the unthinkable. Sometimes defining your bottom line can itself provide a sense of relief. No relationship is worth damaging your mental or physical well-being.

Chapter Six

Sadomasochism in the Workplace

No one can make you feel inferior without your consent.

ELEANOR ROOSEVELT

The workplace is fertile ground for breeding masochism and sadomasochistic relationships. Binds, sabotages, and torments are commonplace. So are the infinite variety of never-ending tangos between foreman and worker, manager and employee, supervisor and subordinate. The workplace lends itself to Everyday Masochism because it is built on power relationships and hierarchies. One person has control and authority over another, and that control and authority may be abused in any number of ways. Personal or professional frustrations may be displaced. Character problems may be played out. Competition and power struggles may encourage backstabbing and duplicitous actions.

There are very few controls on interpersonal excesses in the workplace. Most sadistic behavior can be rationalized as managerial prerogative or tough business practice. As long as pro-

141

duction or efficiency does not appear to suffer directly, tyranny is unlikely to be checked. Those in authority are generally given a great deal of leeway when it comes to social relations.

Many companies, in fact, have their own neurotic style, and their business practices reflect their "pathology" at every level. Using the terminology of psychiatric nomenclature, organizational researchers Manfred Kets de Vries and Danny Miller have identified five different kinds of troubled companies: dramatic, depressive, paranoid, compulsive, and schizoid. They contend that the strategy, structure, and organizational climate of a business mirrors the neuroses of its top echelon. Managers of a depressive company, for example, create an environment characterized by feelings of guilt, worthlessness, self-reproach, loss of interest and motivation, and a sense of helplessness. A paranoid organization's executives—themselves hypersensitive and distrustful of others—foster an atmosphere of suspicion and overconcern for hidden motives. Managers of a dramatic enterprise establish a climate earmarked by bold decisions, impulsive risk-taking, and self-aggrandizing actions.

If the organizational style of a corporation is itself pathological, every employee relationship will inevitably be affected by that pathology. Schizoid organizations will promote cool, detached relationships. Compulsive companies will breed dominance and submission. Dramatic corporations will alternate between idealization and devaluation of their employees. And so on. It is not hard to imagine how the character of the tangos and torments at a particular workplace will be defined by the specific neurotic processes that run amok there.

For example, Kets de Vries and Miller point to one dramatic company whose grandiose and flamboyant CEO set the tone for all operations. He kept his top executives busy "supplying him with trivial information, and he questioned—even scolded—them when they failed to consult him on decisions." The man's desire for attention and visibility, and his need to show how really great an executive he was, obstructed communication. It also created passivity and fear among middle-level managers who slavishly adhered to the procedures he laid down.

Even if you work for a "healthy" organization, the high level of stress created by emphasis on performance and profit tends to create circumstances that bring out either your best or worst. It is not uncommon for an individual with latent sadism to express his hidden tendencies exclusively in the workplace. The Everyday Masochist may also be inspired by the atmosphere in the office to sabotage and torment himself beyond usual limits. Work presents specific problems to each EM type, and the torments and binds in which they are likely to be ensnared are different, too.

Perfectionists

As employees, perfectionists are often preoccupied with details. They are very good at exacting work but usually miss the big picture. They tend to be dogmatic and maintain a love affair with rules that they follow to the letter. In fact, they know the procedure manuals by heart and are sticklers for exact compliance. They can be stubborn and obstinate, requiring all those over whom they wield authority to do it their way. They are generally unimaginative, too focused on minutiae to contemplate the brilliant and innovative.

Because they exercise a great deal of control over themselves and all that they do, perfectionists tend to be difficult people to work for. They won't allow a free flow of ideas, and spontaneity is not their strong suit. On the other hand, they are just the right person to follow through on someone else's concept. They are good at task completion and generally work hard to meet deadlines although their perfectionism usually prevents them from finishing a job quickly.

They are not pragmatic workers. On the contrary, they tend toward inflexibility so that when the unexpected arises, they often behave like the proverbial canoeist without a paddle. Their need for perfection creates indecision. Because they are afraid of making an error they'll sit on a situation that requires immediate action. They are fearful of change and may covertly resist organizational restructuring or personnel changes. Examples:

Carol was a regional sales manager for a growing semi-conductor manufacturer. She lived by the regulations and, in fact, co-authored the procedures manual for the company. She was a marketing genius of sorts, but her sales staff detested her. They objected to her complete reliance on formal rules and her inability and unwillingness to talk to them about their complaints. "Put it in writing" was her oft-repeated phrase. As a result, her department suffered from low morale, high rates of absenteeism, and continual, covert sabotage.

John was a middle-level manager in charge of administering the health plan of a moderately sized, rather conservative manufacturing company whose business practices were highly routinized. When the company was absorbed by a large, free-wheeling conglomerate, he had great difficulty making the transition. Used to following standardized, formal policies, he did not work well in an environment that rewarded venturesome, audacious risk-taking and high-profile, opinionated executives. He sought specific direction from his superiors, and when they responded by encouraging him to suggest and initiate new ideas, he was bewildered. Eventually, he left the company.

Favorite Torments

CALAMITIZING: The job is an ideal place for the perfectionist to engage in contemplating disaster. Many opportunities present themselves for internal statements such as "What if the boss doesn't like my proposal," "What if I screw up at the meeting," "What if I don't finish on time."

SCREENING: Perfectionists search for the flaw in their performance and then dwell on it. Because they set idealized standards for themselves, finding a soft spot is almost inevitable. A patient of mine, for example, did an excellent job preparing an extended marketing plan but had difficulty constructing the projected sales tables for it. She thought of her effort as marginal because all she could see were the weaknesses in her projected figures. She was taken by surprise when the plan got good reviews.

PROJECTING CRITICISM: With annual evaluations now common managerial practice, perfectionists have a formal assessment process to worry about. Not that they need additional worries. They tend to see criticism everywhere: in the boss's coolness at the Christmas party; in the indifferent reception to their last progress report; in recommendations for how they might meet their new sales quotas. Anything less than unqualified praise is interpreted negatively.

FEDERAL OFFENSES: Exaggerating the importance of one's mistakes is another common torment. To the perfectionist, an innocent collating error becomes grounds for demotion. A single incidence of lateness is seen as ruining one's reputation. Failure to observe company protocol is interpreted as reason for dismissal.

MUSTERBATIONS: Most popular ironclad rules for behavior at the workplace: I should always be at my best; I should not make any mistakes; I should always follow procedures; I should be the perfect employee.

Pleasers

Because pleasers are obsessed with approval, they tend to be hard workers, cooperative, and well-meaning. Gaining the approbation of their colleagues and avoiding the censure of the boss is their modus operandi. These tendencies, however, are not without their problems. Pleasers are usually yes-men and -women. They ride on the prevailing winds and are swept up by the strongest tides. They won't risk saying what they really think, particularly when it is unpopular, and they view interpersonal caution as both a necessity and a virtue. They don't want to chance disapproval so they shy away from decision making and almost never challenge authority figures. In fact, they are intimidated by authority and are panicked by the boss's scrutiny.

Pleasers are poor limit-setters. They will take on more work than they can handle simply because they feel uncomfortable (guilty) saying "no." Indeed, telling the boss to stop laying it on so heavy is the hardest challenge one can give them. They are afraid of reprimands, put-downs, and the loss of approval. Because they give too much, pleasers inevitably suffer burnout. They become exhausted and disgruntled with the very job they had once liked so well. Afraid of how others might view their emotional fatigue, they keep it hidden, usually blaming themselves for lack of perseverance.

These individuals typically experience a great deal of performance anxiety. They shun the limelight for fear they will humiliate themselves publicly through error or misjudgment. They often blame themselves for other workers' failures and may even point out their own inadequacies in front of their peers. "If I were only a faster typist, we could have had this report out," is a typical refrain. Never mind that the boss took two weeks to write the thing and left only half a day for typing.

Pleasers do a lot of worrying about the impression they make on their co-workers. They sometimes spend too much time making points and too little time making sales. In fact, looking good in the boss's eyes can become such a preoccupation that other aspects of performance may suffer. Examples:

Shirley works as a production manager in the advertising department of an internationally known cosmetics firm. Her boss, usually a strong, hard-driving, no-nonsense type, has been severely depressed following the death of her youngest daughter. In the vacuum created by the boss's absence, the department has become factionalized. Two managers are competing for power and they have succeeded in dividing the staff into two opposing camps. Not wanting to offend either group, Shirley anxiously tries to show allegiance to both sides. Her equivocation produces an unwanted result: She is accepted by neither group and regarded with suspicion by both.

Harvey is editor of a small monthly trade publication. His job includes writing, editing, graphics, layout—just about everything but printing. The task is enormous and he is frequently exhausted by his labors, often working fourteen hours a day and some weekends. When his boss suggests they expand the magazine's format, Harvey argues against the change on editorial and commercial grounds. Not wanting to lose the boss's goodwill, he refuses to tell him he is already overtaxed and cannot handle any increase in his work load. When the new changes are instituted, he becomes ill and is forced to take a leave of absence.

Favorite Torments

MASQUERADING: Most pleasers believe they are phonies whose charade will sooner or later be found out. No matter how many sales quotas they meet or successful meetings they run, they always find a way to neutralize their triumphs. They typically attribute their success to luck, timing, or personal charm, but never to their ability. And, ironically, the more the boss sings their praises, the more anxious they feel about continuing to pull the wool over her eyes.

MEASURING DOWN: Pleasers silently compare themselves with everyone else in the board or coffee room and almost always come out smelling like week-old roses: her deskmate is a better stenographer; her co-worker has written a better report; her colleague is a better public speaker. The individual can more easily perceive the value in someone else's efforts than in her own.

PROJECTING CRITICISM: Reading criticism into perfectly innocent statements or actions is not just a characteristic of the perfectionist. Pleasers do it, too. When the head of a commercial art department sent back a drawing to one of her designers telling him to reduce its size, he immediately assumed she wasn't happy with his effort. Later, he found out that her actions were based exclusively on space requirements, not on the quality of his work. Attributing negative judgments to others without having any basis in fact tells us that pleasers are projecting their own self-critical feelings onto the boss, co-workers, and associates.

DISCOUNTING: Any aspect of work that the pleaser associates with herself is considered second-rate. If a pleaser writes a proposal, she'll tend to view it as nothing special because she wrote it. If she's promoted to a certain managerial level, suddenly that level is insignificant in the larger scheme of things. If she works for a particular department, she'll perceive it as less important than others within the organization. Pleasers have problems estimating their own efforts fairly. And anything with which they identify is similarly devalued.

MUSTERBATIONS: I should be liked by everyone at work; I should try harder, give more; I should be all smiles and good cheer; I should never rock the boat.

Martyrs

Whether these individuals are hard workers or simply complainers, they always act as if they are giving their life's blood to the company. They are generally self-righteous about their efforts, and, in fact, the cynic might suspect they seek out victimizing circumstances in order to languish in the sanctimony they provide.

Martyrs always feel unappreciated on the job. No one quite understands the stress and strain they have suffered working on that late-night report or putting up with the tyrannical boss. No one is really aware of how hard it is for them even to get up in the morning and arrive at work on time. They feel sorry for themselves and often bitterly compare their job situation to what they regard as the more favorable circumstances of someone else.

Their self-pity immobilizes them, preventing efforts to improve things. For example, they won't remind their boss that a particular task is outside their job description but they will gripe about the extra work to co-workers. Or they won't question a negative job evaluation but will ruminate for weeks about its unfairness.

Their anger smolders within and generally emerges indirectly. They may assume an abrupt and unpleasant tone with their superiors. They may play an obstructionist role at meetings. They may sabotage a person or project through vindictive gossip or the distortion of facts. They may even try to fractionalize the workplace. What they will not do is directly confront the issue they feel strongly about. All of their circuitous actions are a response to the built-up anger they are afraid to express.

At the same time, martyrs exaggerate just how badly they have it. Indeed, they may be working no harder than their boss or anyone else in the company, but this fact doesn't compute. They are overfocused on their own situation. In addition to their feelings of being victimized by circumstances and people, they have a false sense of self-importance. They feel they should receive special consideration although they would never risk asking for it outright. For this reason, they are not effective team players and function best on their own. Examples:

For six years Leonard has worked for the state government determining eligibility for welfare benefits. When a new supervisor proposes procedural changes in the department, Leonard is strongly opposed. He gripes and groans to his co-workers but says nothing at the general meeting held to discuss the proposal. After the changes are adopted, he stubbornly resists them. He delays filing required paperwork, fails to collect data to evaluate the new system, and generally sabotages efficiency by bad-mouthing the plan.

When Sandra is passed up for a promotion, she feels mistreated and resentful. Although the employee who got the job was the logical choice with five more years' seniority and better experience, she overlooks these facts. Noticing only that she has been personally rejected, Sandra silently nurses feelings of betrayal. When her boss questions her sullenness, she denies anything is wrong.

Favorite Torments

GROUCHING: As Leonard and Sandra demonstrate, office martyrs come in two varieties: murmuring malcontents and silent sufferers. The first group engages in this torment by using the office as a sounding board to express grievances to everyone but the person who should hear them: the boss is working the staff too hard; a coworker is callous and insensitive; the building is a cauldron in summer; the elevators are too crowded. Grouching is the avocation of these individuals and their work usually suffers because of all the time they spend bellyaching about what's wrong.

PERSONALIZING: The boss doesn't say "good morning" in the hall; the individual's name is mistakenly excluded from a list of employees with accrued sick leave; they are the last ones to receive an invitation to the company picnic. All these events are interpreted, not as inadvertent occurrences, but as intentional messages specifically directed to them: they are out of favor with the boss; the clerk who calculates sick leave doesn't like them; they are not really wanted at the picnic. Overinterpreting the meaning of random or inconsequential events in the workplace is another way martyrs create needless suffering.

GLOBALIZING: Martyrs are so likely to expect the worst that they often draw catastrophic conclusions from a single incident. For example, a friend in the software duplication business failed to sign a major client after weeks of effort. She confided to me that her career was over. She had failed to land the "big one," everyone would know, and her reputation would plummet. Yet although she lost the client her expectations of doom never materialized. In another instance, when the furniture factory a patient of mine worked for was acquired by a large conglomerate, he predicted dire consequences. "We'll all be fired, and in this economy I'll never find a another job. I'm sure my wife will leave me," he groaned. As it turned out, he didn't lose his job and the business tripled in size after the merger.

MUSTERBATIONS: Martyrs are more interested in how other people *should* behave toward them than in ironclad rules for themselves. Their list looks like this: I should never be treated unfairly by those in authority; I should always be appreciated for my efforts; I should never be inconvenienced by other people; I should always get what I want.

Avoiders

Avoiders are inconsistent workers. Sometimes they are positively brilliant, other times lackluster and mediocre. The problem rests in their heightened ambivalence. They are uncertain whether they want to succeed or not, just as they are confused about what they want from their lives in general. They are absent or late from work a great deal, and they tend to procrastinate.

Avoiders fear success for many reasons. Some are afraid it will bring loneliness and provoke hostility from the envious. Others fear it will create overly high expectations or transform them into ruthless megalomaniacs. Still others feel they don't deserve success, or that it would mean the loss of pleasure in their lives.

Whatever the motive, avoiders are poor decision makers. They will go to great lengths to postpone important choices and make all sorts of excuses to themselves or their superiors. "I don't have enough data," "I couldn't fit it into my tight schedule," "I'm studying the problem," and "I think we need to move cautiously" are the usual excuses.

Typically, the avoider will defer any action that involves confrontation or the possibility of an exchange of feeling. As managers, they are particularly uncomfortable evaluating their subordinates and may behave perfunctorily or formally in order to spare themselves the possibility of genuine interaction. They are uncomfortable with disagreement on any level because it may lead to outright conflict and the expression of anger. For this reason, they generally make good peacemakers and poor advocates.

Avoiders prefer a low profile and tend to work quietly without fanfare; they neither relish nor seek the spotlight. They are seldom effective leaders and perform better in companies where procedures are formalized and established. They do poorly in organizations that are adventuresome, bold, intuitive, and emotionally expressive.

Sabotage runs high in this group. Unconscious fear of success results in strong starts and weak finishes, critical errors, and serious misjudgments. Examples:

Terry has been in sales all his working life but has never settled comfortably into one job. Two years is about the longest he has stayed with a single employer. In his latest effort—selling medical supplies to hospitals—he starts off like a house afire. His first-half sales are triple that of every other person in the organization and his boss has great hopes for him. In the third quarter, however, he inexplicably stops producing, and by the end of the year his numbers are only slightly above average.

Rhoda works for a small printing company that has big growth ideas. As part of its expansion, the business has won a contract with the local professional baseball team to print the club's yearbook. Rhoda is put in charge of the project. She has never handled anything this big before and she feels uncertain of herself. Instead of moving rapidly to meet the team's firm deadline, she finds numerous reasons to delay. The result? She is overwhelmed at deadline and the quality of the job suffers accordingly. She makes excuses by blaming her failure on a time frame that was unrealistic (although she made it so).

Favorite Torments

TAKEAWAY: The fundamental rule is: If you give or get something pleasurable, you must also take something away. For avoiders, this is generally an unconscious process that looks like this: The boss compliments you on your managerial abilities. You bask in the praise for a few moments, then suspect him of setting you up to take on extra work. Or you give yourself a twenty-minute "stress break" to soothe your nerves and end up working an hour and a half overtime to make up for it.

SABOTAGE: Because avoiders put off facing circumstances, they do not torment themselves with the same frequency as the other EM styles. Much of their suffering takes the form of unconscious sabotage brought on by unknown fears. Failing to return important phone calls, showing up late for a crucial meeting, neglecting to put critical information in a report are typical of the kind of traps avoiders are likely to fall into at work.

MUSTERBATIONS: I should be successful but not too successful; I should let sleeping dogs lie; I should never express strong feelings; I should mind my own business; I should be cautious and not take chances.

ARE YOU IN A SADOMASOCHIST TANGO WITH YOUR BOSS?

The workplace is a highly interactive environment where power and authority are not shared equally. For this reason, the office can be a dance floor for the Sadomasochist Tango. If you suspect you're dancing with the boss, take this short test (answer yes or no):

1. My boss doesn't give an open ear to my opinions and ideas.
2. My boss patronizes me.
3. I find it difficult to speak up when my boss asks my opinion.
4. My boss makes disparaging comments about my appearance and work habits.
5. I feel I should do whatever the boss says.
6. When my boss is having a bad day, sooner or later, he'll take it out on me.
7. I have a hard time saying "no" to my boss.
8. My boss has stolen my ideas without giving me credit.
9. If I have a personal problem I don't feel my boss will be understanding.

10. My boss always has to be right.
11. My boss ridicules my mistakes.
12. I feel anxious around my boss.
13. The truth is I'm scared of my boss.
14. I can't trust my boss to keep her word.
15. I feel I have no right to assert my personal needs at work.

If you answered "yes" on four to seven of these questions, there's good reason to believe you're in a tango with your boss. Seven to ten, you've got some real problems that need immediate attention. Over ten, you're in big trouble and won't last long. Start reading the want ads.

Because of the power differential, most tangos are unidirectional. That is, the boss is exclusively in the sadistic role. However, on occasion the situation is reversed. When that happens with any frequency, the boss is likely to be perceived as unable to handle authority (meaning: he can't control subordinates) and will probably be transferred or unemployed shortly.

The characteristics of the Sadomasochist Tango in the workplace mimic those in personal life. There is a chronic pattern of domination. Suffering is imposed by the dominant partner. And there is collaboration and voluntary submission by the subordinate who usually feels resigned.

The six sadistic styles we identified in Chapter 5—exploiters, double-dealers, adversaries, invalidators, fault-finders, and tyrants—can be found at the office as well. In fact, the categories fit bosses with greater precision than they do lovers, teachers, parents, or friends.

Instant Sadomasochism

Consider some of the typical one-liners sadistic bosses use to put down employees. Some are subtly demeaning, others are as obvious as a kick to the groin. Still others are outrightly sexist.

> "You're so cute when you get angry."
> "You probably won't be able to understand this but . . ."
> "It must be that time of month again."
> "Sorry, we've only invited the best minds in the company."
> "How old did you say you were?"
> "I found your report . . . well, interesting."
> "You did take English in high school?"
> "You know, your smile reminds me of my wife's."

One-liners are not the only form of instant S/M the boss uses. The nonverbal gesture is equally powerful in evoking a sense of helplessness in the subordinate. It has immediacy and impact. Words, for all their variety and nuance, are symbols that have to be decoded, and their sting is deadened in the process. Most of the time we react more to the intonation in voice or the physical expression than to the words themselves. If someone smiles and says in a calm manner that he is angry, we are not likely to get too ruffled. Similarly, if he looks furious but says all is forgiven, we will undoubtedly suspect his sincerity. As a general rule, nonverbal messages speak louder than words.

Below I have listed a few of the nonverbal put-downs and intimidations found in the work environment. You know you've got a problem if you chronically find yourself in any of these uncomfortable circumstances.

> The boss ignores you or doesn't bother to look up from her desk when you ask a question.
> While lecturing you, the boss jabs you repeatedly with a rigid finger.
> The boss gives you the silent treatment for several days in a row.

The boss slaps his forehead with the heel of his palm in reaction to your latest suggestion.
The boss turns her back on you while addressing the rest of the group.
The boss leans over your desk and glares down at you. You get the impression it would be improper to get up and view him eye to eye.
The boss closes her eyes whenever you speak at meetings.

SHALL WE DANCE?

Here are some typical tangos from the workplace.

Work Tango 1: Promises, Promises

TYPICAL DANCERS: Double-dealers and martyrs.

THE DANCE: The boss promises to upgrade her subordinate's salary if he will do some after hours work to bail her out of a tight situation. When the time comes for the promotion, she denies she has made such an arrangement. The same day she asks her employee in confidence to provide some personal information about someone else in the office. Several weeks later she makes that information public, seriously embarrassing her subordinate.

The employee's response to both actions is to behave helplessly. He complains to his coworkers about his supervisor's lack of integrity but does nothing to confront her with her double-dealing. He doesn't remind her that he gave her information in confidence, and he refuses to pursue the promotion issue even as a miscommunication that needs to be set straight. Instead, he feels sorry for himself, pouts, and complains about being taken advantage of.

THE DANCE STEPS: She lies and violates confidences; he remains passive and feels victimized; repeat.

Work Tango 2: Treat 'em Like Dirt

TYPICAL DANCERS: Tyrants and pleasers.

THE DANCE: The manager struts around the office as if he owns it. He treats his subordinates like lackeys. His favorite tactic is to stand over an employee's desk and scrutinize her behavior from on high. He is also fond of putting his face several inches from someone else's ear and speaking in a loud, histrionic manner. Everyone in his department tries to stay out of his way, but he picks on just those individuals who seem most intimidated by him. He likes to use rough language and is fond of threatening his subordinates with such blustering lines as: "If the job isn't done on time, heads will roll"; "This company doesn't keep people who are incompetent"; "Anyone leaving early need not come back the next day."

Although the pleaser knows other people are intimidated, she generally assumes she has been singled out above all others for special abuse. She feels extremely anxious when the boss is around and the quality of her work suffers, leaving her more vulnerable to his attacks. As always, her response is to be acquiescent and sweet. She says "good morning" in the most hangdog, submissive manner; greets him with a saccharine smile; and generally pretends he is not the dictator everyone knows him to be. Far from being won over by her actions, the boss is more contemptuous. He starts to pick on her with cruel frequency. Unable or unwilling to perceive the effect of her actions, she continues her behavior until she in fact becomes the favored target of his aggression.

THE DANCE STEPS: He intimidates, she is submissive; he is provoked, she appeases; repeat.

Work Tango 3: Picky, Picky

TYPICAL DANCERS: Faultfinders and perfectionists.

THE DANCE: The supervisor is always complaining about her subordinates' efforts. If they submit a report, she finds fault with the content. If they change the content, she finds an error in the grammar. They correct the grammar, she doesn't like the paper the report is written on. No effort is appreciated. When a particular employee applies for a job in another department, she gives him a reference that is filled with faint praise and left-handed compliments. She subtly questions his abilities and ignores his accomplishments.

Instead of seeing her actions as a style of response, he takes the criticism to heart. He begins to think of himself as a poor worker, "not managerial material," "a man without real talent." He castigates himself for his inadequate performance and ruminates about getting fired. Rather than question the accuracy of her judgments or ask for a meeting to discuss her evaluation, he sets out to meet what he imagines are her expectations. He starts by coming in early, plugging away through lunch, and even working at home. But it makes no difference how hard he tries, his supervisor continues to pick at him.

THE DANCE STEPS: She criticizes, he doubts himself and tries harder; repeat.

Work Tango 4: Whose Idea Is This Anyway?

TYPICAL DANCERS: Exploiters and avoiders.

THE DANCE: The manager asks his assistant for her ideas on a new project. She gives his request a lot of thought and presents him with a detailed memo. At a meeting the next day, he presents her report without acknowledging her authorship.

When he hears that word of the incident has gotten back to her, he assures her that he has every intention of giving her full credit, but that the meeting would have been an inappropriate place. Weeks go by without any action on his part. The matter fades into memory. Months later he makes a similar request and again steals her ideas without acknowledgment.

The assistant plays into the dance by denying that her boss could actually be exploiting her. She makes excuses for him: "He carries a lot of responsibility, and this unimportant matter just slipped his mind." She downplays the significance of his actions by demeaning the quality of her ideas: "They were just a few trivial suggestions anyway." And she even rationalizes his behavior as "just what happens in big organizations." Even when his exploitation is obvious to everyone else in the office, she continues to deny his true motives.

THE DANCE STEPS: He uses her, she rationalizes his behavior; repeat.

Work Tango 5: Sex in the Office

TYPICAL DANCERS: Exploiters and pleasers.

THE DANCE: The boss is a male chauvinist who makes demeaning sexual comments to women subordinates and treats them with little respect. He flirts with the attractive women in the office and has a reputation for promoting employees in whom he's romantically interested. He is particularly taken with one of the young women in the typing pool. He spends half the day hanging around the general vicinity of her desk and can be heard making bawdy, inappropriate jokes. In fact, he has frequently suggested that a liaison with him would be worth her while.

Although the young subordinate does not show an eagerness to take up his request, she is cordial and all smiles. She doesn't really like him and is uncomfortable with his sexual innuendos and excessive attentions, but she is also fearful of the consequences if she expresses her real feelings. Uncertain of how to act, she allows him to take more and more liberties. His ogling and occasional touching are especially debasing. Still, she plays along with him, afraid a confrontation will cost her his favor and perhaps her job.

THE DANCE STEPS: He flirts, she is non-committal; he escalates, she fails to set limits; repeat.

Work Tango 6: One Up, One Down

TYPICAL DANCERS: Adversaries and martyrs.

THE DANCE: The supervisor is a know-it-all who talks incessantly at meetings, showing off the breadth and scope of his knowledge and giving no one else a chance to speak. One of his preferred sports is to ask a question of his staff and then demonstrate that only he knows the real answer. He is pompous, self-inflated, and a real bore. A subordinate tries to get a word in, and she is cut off like a car in commuter traffic.

The subordinate's reaction is to sulk and withdraw into herself. She feels dismissed and personally slighted, although her boss acts this way toward everyone. She thinks of herself as the only employee who has ever had a difficult or frustrating supervisor. She ruminates about her bad luck in being assigned to this department. Gradually her self-pity takes its toll on her work and motivation.

THE DANCE STEPS: He puffs himself up by cutting her down, she feels personally victimized and resentful; repeat.

WHAT TO DO AND WHAT NOT TO DO IF YOU'RE IN A TANGO

If these tangos strike a chord, consider the response guidelines below:

"Don'ts"

- Don't sulk and withdraw.
- Don't indulge in self-pity.
- Don't give up and passively accept the situation.
- Don't quit.
- Don't try to get the boss fired.
- Don't waste energy complaining.

In a study of intolerable bosses, organizational researchers Michael Lombardo and Morgan McCall found that employees who tried to get the boss fired were almost always unsuccessful. The boss's authority and influence were too great for an individual in a subordinate position to combat. Lombardo and McCall also found that many employees believed that no active strategy improved matters, and that an attitude of viewing the situation as a learning experience was helpful.

My own research indicates that, unlike most other relationships where direct confrontation can be helpful, it is usually counterproductive here. Patient and well-conceived strategies have more lasting and positive effects.

"Dos"

Below are some additional guidelines that will help you deal more effectively with each sadistic type.

- Take stock of the situation. Make a realistic assessment. When does the boss behave sadistically? Does he or she act the tyrant with everyone? What provokes the boss? How do others successfully handle the situation?

• Determine the boss's sadistic style. Is he or she a fault-finder, tyrant, invalidator?

• Evaluate what you are doing to feed into the S/M system. Are you too compliant, passive, negative, oppositional? Do you allow the boss to overstep professional boundaries without protest? Do you send out nonverbal messages that you are intimidated or incompetent? Are you trying too hard to win the boss's approval and respect?

• Devise a defensive strategy based on the sadistic style of the boss. Here are some examples:

DOUBLE DEALERS: If they exploit personal confidences, keep your relationships on a strictly business level. If promises are made, get them in writing or make sure a third person is present. Recognize their unscrupulousness and don't make excuses for them.

TYRANTS: Don't show you are intimidated. Nothing attracts them more than vulnerability. Keep your relationships professional and your interactions brief. Don't talk about extraneous issues. Never be self-critical in their presence. Don't justify or defend your opinions or actions unless you are asked to. Stay out of their way as much as possible.

EXPLOITERS: If they overwork you, set limits. Call attention to your job duties and work hours as defined in your job description. Be persistent. Don't feel guilty for protecting your own interests. Be generous only if your generosity is honestly appreciated. Don't let your goodwill be manipulated.

ADVERSARIES: If they must always have the upper hand, use their ego to your advantage. Outright flattery is too obvious, but it is helpful to link your new ideas with theirs. For example, begin a statement with "I'd like to make a suggestion based on what you said yesterday." Join with the narcissistic ego to make room for yourself.

FAULTFINDERS: As hard as it is, don't take their attempts at humiliation personally. Reframe their actions as "letting off steam." See it as the boss's problem. He is looking to make someone a scapegoat and you are the current target. When the time seems right, ask him for *specific* suggestions to help your performance. Often this will move him from a diatribe to a constructive response.

INVALIDATORS: Be alert. They are insidious sadists whose put-downs are subtle enough to miss but powerful enough to undermine. Short circuit their actions by asking for clarification of the ambiguous statement or gesture. But don't ask for support or reveal self-doubts in front of them.

• Devise an offensive strategy:

LOOK FOR AREAS OF MUTUALITY: Build a more positive relationship by talking about issues of joint interest. Search for common ground, shared values, and a reciprocal outlook.

ACCEPT THE BOSS AS THE BOSS: This doesn't mean accepting everything the boss does, only the fact that he or she has authority. A boss who feels his or her power is threatened may behave in an unpredictable and vindictive manner. Remember, you are not in a power struggle as such with your superior. Clearly your boss has the power. You *are* in a struggle to maintain your integrity and do your job under difficult conditions.

TIMING IS IMPORTANT: Whenever possible, make contact when the boss is not preoccupied or in a bad mood. It is not advantageous to meet with him or her directly after the company's dismal third-quarter results have been released. Likewise, if you know your boss is cranky in the morning, schedule meetings in the afternoon. Also keep in mind your own mental condition and optimum periods of functioning.

ENCOUNTER THE BOSS: Sometimes it is best to simply bring the entire S/M relationship into the open, though this strategy is not for everyone. You must have a sense (historical knowledge is even better) that the boss can be reasonable and receptive to honest and direct dialogue. Pick a positive moment after a period of relative calm in the relationship. Speak straightforwardly and without exaggeration. Be firm about your position but not stubborn. And don't blame. Nothing provokes a defensive response more than blaming. Instead of saying "I can't stand your constant criticism," use a more positive approach, such as "I work better when I feel supported or encouraged," or simply "I don't feel as supported as I'd like." "I" statements work better than "you" statements. The former imply you are taking individual responsibility; the latter sound as if you are casting blame.

KEEP PERSPECTIVE: The workplace is a fluid environment. Things change. People move on. You won't have this boss forever. Keep in mind that you work for the company and not your immediate superior.

DEFINE YOUR OWN LIMITS: What is your tolerance level? How bad do things have to get before you bail out? It is important to define your personal bottom line and respect it. And that line can vary greatly between people. For many of the individuals I interviewed, the red flag was when their work relationships seriously impaired other aspects of their lives. They were likely to leave their job, for example, if they felt their marriage was deteriorating under the strain of an S/M tango at work.

STAY RELAXED: It is never easy to suffer fools or tyrants, but if one must, it is helpful to stay calm and at ease. Maintaining a pragmatic attitude alone is not enough. If you are in a tango, you need all your resources. Slow down. Put aside twenty minutes of the workday for meditation or stress-reduction exercises. Practice deep abdominal breathing while you are at your desk. Don't underestimate the connection between anxiety and physical tension.

LEARN FROM THE TANGO: As mentioned earlier, it is helpful to view the S/M relationship as a learning experience. If nothing else, it will help you to appreciate the next boss. Beyond this there are lessons in dealing with adversity, resolving conflict, appreciating and respecting your own limits, and conquering frustration and anxiety. Above all, there is the negative lesson of "how not to be" a boss. By viewing others' mistakes and feeling the pain of their errors, we can learn to become managers who treat people with humanity and respect.

CALL FOR MEDIATION OR ARBITRATION: If the situation is impossible to tolerate and the company has a mediation or arbitration process, use it. Bring in a third party to help you work through your grievances or decide a deadlocked issue. Sometimes only an individual who is not a part of the system has the clarity and neutrality to recognize and have an impact on the tango. If you do use a third party, insist on confidentiality and be prepared to back up your claims with facts.

BAIL OUT: If all else fails, look for an opportunity to transfer within the organization or, if this is impossible, leave the company. Not every job is worth the cost in personal aggravation, stress, and lost self-esteem. Remaining in an intolerable situation may be masochistic. Respect your limits and the feedback you get from friends and intimates. A well-paid job may be hard to find, but ill health, a lost relationship, or depression are hardly worth the price.

Chapter **Seven**

Anatomy of a Masochist

*Language which does not acknowledge the
body cannot acknowledge life.*

JOHN LAHR

The human body is a road map to the psyche. Its tension, posture, energy, and movement tell us what lies in the territory within. Our emotional history can be charted on the lines of our faces; our deepest sensitivities are revealed in our eyes. We can observe from a person's walk whether he or she is disillusioned and burdened by life or ecstatic and joyful. We can see defeat and resignation in posture as well as pride and determination. We have only to read the map.

Muscular tension patterns are particularly revealing. In early childhood, muscles are flexible and movement is free, without constriction. As an individual progresses through life, tension patterns become more fixed, influenced by the interacting factors of aging and environment. If the child is raised in a fearful and threatening environment, for example, the body as well as the psyche will reflect those conditions. The child will become distrustful, withdrawn, and fearful of intimacy in adulthood. Since every emotional event is also a physical event, the person will show a high state of chronic tension, particularly in the muscles surrounding the small joints of the body.

Unless something is done to intervene, the chronic tension will persist throughout life. It will become second nature the way a particular manner of walking or talking becomes second nature. And only when required to move in unfamiliar ways, or when life stress is excessive, will he or she become aware of the pattern's existence.

Because the psychological beginnings of all Everyday Masochists share some common characteristics, we might expect muscle tension patterns to be similar. And they are. Although there may be great variety in the size and shape of their bodies, EMs typically store tension in the neck and throat muscles. The tension can often be palpated, but it is most easily observed in the voice, which is restricted and controlled. They have been conditioned to hold back their feelings, particularly anger, and this suppression has been accomplished by tensing the area around the voice path.

A patient of mine who scored high on the EM scale had a rather strong and brassy speaking voice. Her elocution was distinguished by a quality of assurance, and her tones were full and powerful. I wondered about this contradiction until one day I heard her scream. Out of her usually overpowering larynx emerged a restricted peep that sounded more like bleating than an expression of distress. Under stress, she reflexively bore down on the muscles surrounding her throat and constrained her voice. She held back at the critical moment just as she had been taught as a child when her parents admonished her to be "seen and not heard."

A second area of masochistic tension is in the pelvis. The muscles in the buttocks are tightly held, and there is a slight forward tilt that somewhat resembles a dog with its tail between its legs. Some body-oriented psychotherapists believe this tension is the result of early or excessively harsh toilet training that led the child to tighten all the muscles in the pelvic region in order to gain continence. The result of this holding pattern is that the pelvis itself is not very mobile and cannot swing freely. Sexual inhibition is also considered a cause of this tension.

The Everyday Masochist feels special vulnerability in the abdomen. I have heard many patients identify it as the seat of their anxiety. As one might suspect, it is also an area characterized by deep tension, a protective response against feeling fear or sadness. A person usually pulls in the belly out of vanity. Masochists do it to feel more secure. Wrapping a region in tension reduces sensation and feeling as blood flow and energy are cut off. You can experiment with this phenomenon by tightening all the muscles in your chest. Notice that the effect is to give you a sense of impenetrability. Your chest feels armored, defended, and all softer or vulnerable feelings are temporarily inaccessible.

The upper back is another area prone to tension. The shoulders are rolled forward and look burdened as if they have been carrying the world. There is often a sense that the individual is holding back (again the expression of anger), and there is deep tension binding the shoulder blades and upper arms.

The legs are also tight. Although they may be strong and particularly developed in the calves, they are somewhat rigid and immobilized by holding patterns, especially in the hamstrings, the posterior muscles of the thighs. This tension may show up in stretching problems with aerobic exercise, difficulty jumping, or muscle cramping after long walks or jogs.

COMPRESSION IMPRESSION

Consider for a moment your own posture. Do you stand upright with your back straight and head erect? Do you lean heavily to one side, favoring a particular leg? Do you arch your back and retract your shoulders? Posture may be idiosyncratic, but it is not random. It makes a statement about who we are. It says we are proud, afraid, arrogant, exhausted, even disillusioned.

Posture may also be evocative. It can create a mood or sustain one. Try this demonstration. From an upright position, let your head slump forward for half a minute. Undoubtedly, you'll begin to feel dejection. Now inhale high into your chest and raise your head upward. Do you feel any difference? Simply moving your head to another position can temporarily change your mood by sending specific cues associated with a particular feeling to the brain. Paul Ekman of the University of California at San Francisco has shown in cross-cultural studies that precise muscle movements are linked to particular emotions. Anger, for example, is expressed in primitive as well as modern societies through lowered and drawn together eyebrows, a hard stare, and tightly compressed lips. Conversely, by assuming facial gestures related to a characteristic emotion, we can elicit feeling, a trick known to every stage actor.

The most outstanding feature of the Everyday Masochist's posture is compression. The individual is collapsed into himself somewhat like an accordion. The compression gives the sense that the person feels defeated, passive, and burdened, all characteristics associated with masochism. It is as if someone has placed a heavy weight on the standing body, causing it to be squeezed downward. The millstone in this case is the burden of following the ironclad requirements that EMs have for themselves; the endless list of hard and fast rules for conduct—the "tyranny of shoulds"—described earlier.

The typical masochist's body collapses into itself at the waist, creating a C-curve posture as the pelvis is drawn forward. There is a submissive quality to this position. Pride,

assertion, and power are missing; self-obstruction, subjuga-
tion, and defeat are suggested.

The compression is an indication of the Everyday Masochists' psychological condition. They have not been allowed
full expression of their autonomy. Their assertion has been
thwarted. Their needs and preferences have taken a backseat
to the desires of those whose approval they reflexively seek.
They have been sat on and now they sit on themselves. Their
compression expresses it all. They collapse rather than reach
out to manipulate the world.

One of my patients wrote this curious description at the
beginning of her therapy:

> I feel like I'm actually getting physically smaller. I was
> sitting in a meeting at work yesterday, comparing myself
> to others in the room and feeling insignificant, when all
> of a sudden I experienced myself as puny. I could feel my
> body literally shrinking into the chair like Alice in
> Wonderland. For a second, I imagined I would disap-
> pear altogether. I felt like a collapsed sack of potatoes
> with no backbone. Even when I sat up straight I still felt
> small."

My patient's heightened body awareness is not atypical.
Many of my clients have reported similar physical sensations
of "caving in," "feeling caught between vice grips," or "being
clamped down." Muscle tension at the top and bottom of the
gastrointestinal tract contributes to this sensation of collapse
and shrinkage. The individual feels as if her very presence is
diminishing. Just the simple action of extending the body,
draping it backward over the arm of a chair or sofa, away from
its chronic flexion, brings a sense of relief and renewal.

HOLDING IT ALL IN

Life energy pulses through all of us. Although the exact nature of that energy is still debated—electrical, biochemical,

cosmic, or divine—there is little disagreement that without it the human organism would cease to function. Energy is synonymous with life and is central to all activities of the living, including moving, feeling, and thinking.

Some organisms have more energy than others. They appear to have greater vitality, endurance, strength, and power. Compare the vigor of record-breaker Pete Rose with the journeyman baseball player. Rose hustles into his third decade of competitive play while the average player retires after only a dozen seasons. The difference is difficult to figure. It is not only a matter of how efficiently an organism converts food into fuel thus creating energy, but also what food is consumed and how well that fuel is utilized. Personality is another variable in the equation. For although energy is a factor in determining the kind of life we live, our personality influences how we use that energy, whether we suppress or express it.

EMs usually have a great deal of energy, but it is stagnant and trapped within their compression. The result, particularly during stress, is a feeling that they are going to burst. An EM is like a whistling teapot with a malfunctioning safety valve. The steam builds up pressure, looks for a way to escape but finds no release. Occasionally, it leaks out (anxiety) but most often it destroys its container from within (psychosomatic disorders).

Everyday Masochists have no way to release frustrations, built-up tensions, and the accumulated wear and tear of life. They find it hard to relax. They have trouble crying deeply (although superficial tears are common enough). They dare not express their backlog of resentments for fear of retaliation. Even on vacation they worry instead of letting go. Their minds are cluttered with tormenting thoughts. They struggle against self-created binds and sabotages. Really, they have no peace.

From an energetic standpoint, the problem of these individuals is that they are high-energy organisms without an adequate way of discharging. Alexander Lowen, the founder of Bioenergetics, has written that masochists try to squeeze out tension instead of relaxing and letting it flow. They push to relax, and in the process clamp down, blocking the very goal they wish to achieve.

> I can't seem to cry. My eyes well up with tears. I feel sadness inside but each time I push myself to the brink, something stops me. I hear a whimper or two and then I shut it off somehow. I can feel the urge to bawl like a baby and although I keep trying as hard as I can, I can't get it out. My whole body feels like a clogged drain. I'm all stuffed up.

These are the words one of my patients used to describe his experience after the death of his father. Although he felt a deep loss, he could not release to the feeling. Typically, he tried to push himself to feel, but increased effort did not help. He needed to surrender to his pain. A lifetime of holding in had made it difficult for him to release. A Zen adage speaks to the point: "You can't take water from a stream with a closed fist."

Wilhelm Reich even went so far as to say that the sexual masochist's inability to achieve release leads him to provoke others to stern measures. In Reich's view the beatings and abuses that the individual urges the sadistic partner to inflict are really attempts at getting the release that could not be achieved alone. The masochist is willing to accept (and even incite) beatings just to get some sort of discharge.

Consider the situation of one of my patients who couldn't get angry. Indeed, he was petrified of expressing the deep, seething resentment he felt toward his hypercritical father. Instead of venting those feelings, he would provoke others to anger, including his girlfriend and boss. In the process, he vicariously experienced his own rage and hours later felt an exquisite sense of relief. It was a circuitous way of attaining catharsis, but it worked for him.

BENEATH THE SMILE

There is no more expressive part of the human anatomy than the face. Flashing eyes, furrowed brow, jutting chin—all communicate the emotion of the moment and the feelings of a lifetime much more eloquently than words. The most subtle of gestures, a slight raising of one eyebrow, for example, can tell us the boss is skeptical and we'd better try another tack. But the emotion that appears on the face is often faint and evanescent. It is mixed with a variety of other facial gestures—such as lip biting, grimacing, or eye blinking—making it more difficult to interpret. All this considered, the greatest obstacle to "reading" the face is not an overabundance of cues; it is the simple fact that people fail to look. Research shows that during common interactions, people do not closely observe each other. They look only to ascertain interest or agreement (their partner's reaction), or to determine the meaning of a pause or change in the flow of dialogue (conversational management). Since the expression of emotion generally lasts less than five seconds, a great deal of communication is missed.

Psychologist Ekman has written that the face is a multi-message system that communicates not only emotion but information about mood, attitude, character, intelligence, attractiveness, age, sex, and race. He has identified three types of messages: "static signs," such as skin color or bone structure; "slow signals," wrinkles or skin texture; and "rapid indications," produced by the movement of facial muscles.

What are the signs on the Everyday Masochist's face? The question is a complex one because of the wide variation in physiognomy and the human predilection to disguise one's real intentions. In fact, EMs are masters of this game. They usually wear a cheerful mask that says "all's right with me and the world." What they really feel is burdened. If you catch them at an off moment, when they are unaware of your presence or too tired to care, their expression will reflect that condition.

All but one of the four masochist types wears a variation on the "all's well" theme. Typically, pleasers are all smiles and good cheer since they are seeking to win love and approval; their congeniality and goodliness suggest they have no malicious intentions. Perfectionists take great care with their physical appearance; their worth is based on their flawlessness and they are usually meticulously groomed. But there is also an expression of effort on their faces that reveals how hard they are trying. Avoiders are a mixed bag; some wear a look of innocence while others seem to be saying, "Don't bring me any bad news." Martyrs are the one exception: They look unhappy, sometimes miserable. Their countenance expresses the singular theme that they have suffered and are suffering still. Or, as one of my martyred patients succinctly put it: "Life is tough and then you die."

The focal point of these facial expressions is the eyes. There is almost always a quality of deep sadness in them (particularly in the perfectionist and pleaser) which suggests that a disconsolate spirit, a lamenting soul lives within. At the same time they are compelling. They draw you in and almost demand sympathy. "Please like me," is the message they convey. In contrast, the eyes of the avoider are vague and tentative. They do not want to see with any clarity or depth, and they most certainly do not want to make contact and risk the emotion of a real encounter. Often they wear a blank expression that suggests "the lights are on but no one is home."

The eyes of the martyr are long-suffering and grievous. They too are sad but not in a compelling manner. They are the eyes of the victim who feels too much self-pity to evoke sympathy. The intentions of those eyes are suspect. They seem self-righteous, hinting that their owner is indulging in suffering for its own sake and holding on to it longer than necessary.

Most Everyday Masochists hold tightly in the masseter muscles surrounding the jaw. The tension pattern is almost reflexive, a direct result of their training in containment and self-restraint. Wanting to voice their deepest feelings as children but fearing the consequences, they suppressed their impulses by literally holding back their mouths from speaking. Over time the pattern becomes set. Lowen has commented on the intense emotion that bursts forth when the jaw muscles are released through direct manipulation. Much of the masochist's unexpressed feelings are bound up in that tension.

MIRROR TERROR

My research and clinical experience show that most Everyday Masochists have negative feelings about their bodies. Ask them and they will report their thighs are too heavy, their breasts too small, their feet too arched, their torso too squat. The number and variety of complaints is endless. The masochists' critical imagination is noteworthy. Just as they are adept at highlighting the imperfections in their characters, so too are they highly effective at identifying the deficiencies in their bodies.

The torments of Chapter 4 are as relevant to their physiques as they are to their psyche. Take screening, for example. EMs will single out the one feature in their faces they don't like and focus their attention on it. When they look in the mirror they will see only a wide nose and miss their beautiful eyes and sensuous mouth. Or they will notice their full hips but not their shapely legs. Their interest is so directed at the imperfection that all perspective is lost and its ugliness is greatly exaggerated. Tell them differently, and with unconscious irony they will fight tenaciously to overestimate their shortcomings.

Measuring down is another chosen torment. A patient of mine compared his body to those of other men each time he went to the beach. Typically, he chose to match himself against only the most muscled and well-proportioned specimens, completely ignoring the overweight flabby types. The comparison naturally left him feeling inadequate.

Body image and self-image go hand in hand. At the root of the problem is a lack of self-acceptance. Everyday Masochists do not fully accept and embrace their identities. Their fault-finding, comparisons, and put-downs of their bodies are all indications of their failure to simply grant themselves the right to be themselves without apology.

PHYSICAL PROBLEMS AND SENSITIVITIES

Research suggests that Everyday Masochism is bad for your physical as well as emotional health. In a recent study conducted by James Schuele and Alan Wisenfeld, negative self-statements (of the kind EMs frequently make) were found to be more biologically arousing than neutral ones. Cardiac level and respiration rates went up when subjects repeated negative self-evaluations to themselves. Apparently, just the process of reminding yourself of your failures, emphasizing past mistakes, pointing out inadequacies, and believing that you will do poorly can raise more than your anxiety level.

Another study, this one at the University of North Carolina, found that self-criticalness in combination with conformity and conscientiousness was linked to high levels of serum cholesterol. Those with elevated scores on a psychological inventory that measured self-criticism and normative behavior had more cholesterol than a similarly matched group. The findings suggest that the self-critical personality may be more prone to heart attacks since high serum cholesterol has been linked to heart disease.

My research shows that individuals with high EM scores visit their physicians no more frequently than those with low scores. The nature of their physical complaints is varied, but they do tend to focus more on gastrointestinal problems. They complain of stomachaches, queasiness, nausea, and cramps whenever they feel nervous or tense. And they are much more likely to suffer from diarrhea or constipation. Lowen believes these problems are due to interference with the natural eating rhythms during childhood. Both forced feeding and the use of food to symbolically give or withdraw love emotionally charge the process of digestion and make it susceptible to distress.

Chapter **Eight**

The Making of an Everyday Masochist

Smothering a child by anxious concern over
every detail of his life, robbing him of all
opportunities to express himself naturally
and to discover the world for himself . . .
may be more crippling than beatings. . . .

DR. KARL MENNINGER

"Our childhood is what we alone have had . . ." wrote John Updike. The uniqueness of our individual experience is uncontestable. Each of us grows up in a garden of petals and thorns, no two gardens alike; we rise both scarred and perfumed. Yet there are similarities in the terrain of these gardens that leave their particular markings on our individuality. To find these configurations and realize their consequences is one job of applied psychology.

The terrain in the masochist's garden varies from culture to culture and family to family, yet despite differing individual experience, some patterns are clearly detectable. Everyday Masochists have these things in common: their independence (the natural movement toward autonomy) was thwarted; their aggression drives were inhibited; they were made to feel a deep sense of guilt; and they suffered from experiences of negation and humiliation that left them feeling uncertain of themselves.

THWARTED INDEPENDENCE

While standing by the ocean's edge one summer I watched a young child playing in the shallow water. She'd run directly toward the ocean, but as soon as she was about to get wet, she'd turn around and prance the other way. A simple game of "you can't catch me" with the ocean as her playmate. As I continued to observe the little girl I began to see that more was involved than this simple game. Each time she danced back to dry land she'd run over to her mother and clutch her legs. After a brief moment she was off again. Finally, to my surprise she headed straight for the water and jumped (sort of) in.

I analyzed the incident this way: The little girl was afraid of the water and the waves yet she wanted to go in, perhaps out of curiosity or just to imitate her older brother already splashing around. She felt insecure with this risky proposition and ran back to her mother to get assurance. Her clutching behavior apparently gave her the security she needed to take the plunge.

The innocent scene illustrates how the child matures into an autonomous adult. Growth does not proceed in a straight line but is usually preceded by a period of insecurity and regression in which the child returns to earlier, less mature behaviors to gain the security needed to move on. Regression followed by growth repeated over and over again.

Given this insight we can understand how the movement toward autonomy in Everyday Masochists is stifled. When the child regresses in order to prepare for the next jump toward independent functioning, her parent reads this as "she is not ready" instead of "she is getting ready." In some cases this is an honest error that, given the child's propensity to regress, could be made by anyone. In others, as we shall soon learn, parents have their own reasons for stifling their children's independence and keeping them from growing up.

The thwarting can occur throughout childhood, but it generally begins toward the end of the second year of life when children are able to walk and are comfortable enough with their abilities to explore the small world around them. Toilet training is introduced during this time, feeding and eating habits begin to change, children start to exhibit willful behavior ("no" is often the favorite word), and strong preferences develop. The baby/child is growing up.

For some parents this is a welcome change, a sign of healthy growth, but for others—masochist-producing parents—this movement toward autonomy is felt as a loss, an inconvenience, or a threat. These parents feel ambivalent about their child's development. They miss the early physical relationship with all its exclusivity and sweetness. They regret the loss of control they used to exercise. Such parents try to keep their child from growing away from them by discouraging the child's initiating behavior, oversupervising choices, and generally restricting actions that assert independence. All this, of course, is performed with the child's "good" in mind. Since an acknowledged and necessary part of parenting is to teach societal values and social rules, excessive direction can be hidden under the guise of conscientious parenting.

By smothering impulses toward independence, parents of Everyday Masochists make it difficult for their children to explore and master the world around them. Rather than feeling the ability to control and direct their environment, EMs feel controlled by it. The world becomes a dangerous place because they have not learned the skills to make it work for them.

On the emotional level, the costs may be even higher. Enforced dependence does not allow the child to mature or develop a healthy sense of self. The child's needs are too closely associated with the parent's, and this vague boundary creates identity confusion.

As an example, consider this letter, sent to Sharon, a college junior. Notice how her mother attempts to undermine her daughter's independent actions and choices. The text appears on one side of the page; on the other, my interpretation of her mother's real message.

The Letter

Dear Sharon,

We were so glad you called on Sunday when you thought you wouldn't be able to. We weren't happy though to hear that you were calling from Mike's apartment. Are you sure he doesn't have another girlfriend—he seemed the type. Oh well, you know best, dear.

I hope you'll reconsider your plans for spring vacation. Uncle George and Aunt Mary don't often have the chance to visit us and they are so looking forward to seeing you.

I was glad to hear about your "A" on the psychology exam. As you know, I've done a lot of reading on the subject and have become something of an expert, especially now that I'm at the Children's Center. More and more of

The Real Message

I doubt your judgment. I don't support your choice of a boyfriend.

Don't be selfish. Accomodate your plans to ours.

I already know what you're just learning.

my time is spent there. They really
need me too. Just yesterday Mr.
Adams, the director, was telling me
about all the changes they're planning
and how happy they are to have my
help.

*Let's talk about my
achievements not
yours.*

Mary Beth is still a disappointment to
her mother. Marge can't say enough
about how upset she is about the
crowd Mary Beth runs around with.
She's going up to visit her this weekend and hopes they will straighten
things out.

*Don't disappoint me
like Mary Beth disap-
points her mother.*

Your father is working hard. It's tax
season you know and as usual, he's
taken on too many clients and isn't
home much. The house feels so empty
without you to talk to.

*I'm lonely and need
you.*

I've been sitting here and looking at
our old drapes and noticing how much
they've aged. Maybe you would go
with me over spring break to pick out
new ones? We always have such a
good time shopping. Maybe we can
find you a new dress, too.

*Give up your plans
for spring break so we
can be together the
way we always were.
I'll make it worth
your while.*

Every time I sit down to write you I
am surprised again that my little girl is
in college.

*You're still my little
girl.*

We miss you very much,
                    Mom

Notice that the letter contains no validation of Sharon's
choices, no encouragement of her independent actions, and

no awareness of her need for separation and autonomy. Her mother undermines her daughter's judgment, evokes guilt to manipulate her behavior, draws attention away from her achievements (to focus on the mother's), and concludes by diminishing her maturity.

INHIBITED AGGRESSION

Aggression, with its ineluctable connection to war and violence, is rarely eulogized as a desirable human trait. We prefer to praise gentleness and moderation as virtues, even though we extol the "winner" who has had to step on a few toes while scrambling to the top. As far as children are concerned, we usually do not accept aggression, especially when we are its target.

Erich Fromm has pointed out that not only is aggression necessary for survival, but it is far from a monolithic phenomenon. It takes many forms and has numerous functions. Aggression can be both benign and malignant, defensive and destructive, conformist or instrumental. Fromm pays particular attention to what he calls self-assertive aggression, which, he says, is healthy aggression in the original meaning of the word, "moving forward toward a goal, without undue hesitation, thought or fear."

Parents of Everyday Masochists tend to restrict the expression of aggression in their children, even its healthy forms. For example, "rough or loud play" is not permitted, talking back is prohibited; strong language is censored. In fact, most demonstrative acts are suppressed. Children are not encouraged to simply tone down; they are sat on, leaving them no room to naturally discharge energy. Females are told they are not being ladylike; males are labeled bullies or roughnecks. The effect is to teach the child to be more passive and to feel that asserting one's own interests is wrong and selfish.

Later, when demands for successful performance are placed on the child, he or she will be caught in a conflict created by two incongruous messages: win and be good.

Control of such negative emotions as anger and jealousy is so managed in the masochistic family system that children are required to suppress them unconditionally. When this happens, they often turn those feelings back on themselves. Because they have been taught that anger is wrong and unacceptable, they must be deplorable for feeling it: "Only a rotten person gets angry, especially at a father who works unselfishly to provide for me." As noted in Chapter 2, this turning in of aggression becomes a prototype for later behavior and leads to self-contempt, denigration, and self-disparagement as a life-style.

One of my patients, a forty-two-year-old stewardess, told this story:

> When I got angry my mother never said a word. She'd just look at me in this steely way as if I was the worst child she had ever laid eyes on. Then she'd banish me to my room with a venom in her voice. I had to sit still in my chair without moving until she came upstairs to free me. . . . She'd never even talk to me about it. Sitting in that chair I felt like the lowest of the low.

A psychiatrist in his mid-forties relayed this account:

> In my family, no one was allowed to be angry at anyone else. Immediately, my father would tell us to apologize for our feelings and make up. This made for some pretty artificial situations. The long-term result was that we learned to go underground with our feelings. Instead of just saying how we felt, there was a lot of sarcasm, senseless debate, and unspoken hostility. My father couldn't pin us down, but our anger got expressed. Even today, our family still relates in this covert way.

Suppressing healthy aggression in the formative years creates practical problems in later life. The most obvious of these is not being able to stand up for yourself. This failure makes for high anxiety when asking the boss for a raise or setting limits on a lover's excesses. There is also the problem of dealing with conflict in relationships. Since some disaccord is inevitable even in the most compatible partnerships, Everyday Masochists are at a distinct disadvantage. We have already noted how they sweep their own emotions under the rug and feel intimidated by their partners' hostility, submitting or withdrawing to appease and mollify.

HUMILIATIONS AND OTHER NEGATIONS

Most Everyday Masochists remember feelings of humiliation from the past. These are heavily charged secrets that are clothed in shame and embarrassment. Rarely are they disclosed to anyone but the closest confidante.

The deepest humiliations are generally experienced before the child's third birthday and are usually beyond the extent of normal memory. They involve violations of personal boundaries and private functions. Typical parents of EMs take too much interest and concern in toilet training, for example. They are overcontrolling, manipulative, and intrusive in "helping" their offspring to achieve continence. Little sensitivity to the child's natural feelings of privacy is shown. A patient in his fifties reported to me that the memory of his mother's excessive concern and public comment on his bowel movements still bothered him. He suspected that a lifelong struggle with constipation originated with his holding back from his anxious and demanding parent.

Alexander Lowen notes that intrusions into the child's sense of bodily privacy create feelings of humiliation and shame. He lays the blame at the caretaker's feet:

The concern which some parents show over the bowel functions of their children stems from their own neurotic feelings of shame about those functions. It is almost impossible to find a masochist who does not have feelings that the functions of discharge—anal, urethral, and genital—are dirty.

Overcontrol of the child's eating habits (particularly in the second year) also evokes feelings of intrusion. Forced feeding, overfeeding, and overregulated scheduling interfere with the child's natural functioning and violate the developing sense of autonomy.

True, parents must of necessity assume a major role in toilet training and feeding, but when that role is overplayed, and distinctly internal and private functions are heavily scrutinized and controlled, a sense of mortification is provoked. One has only to try force feeding or interfering with the elimination process of a domestic animal to understand the terrible sense of violation that the young human child experiences.

Humiliations are not limited to the areas of feeding and toilet training. Parental mockery, disrespect, ridicule, and indifference are humiliating to a child's fragile sense of self. Adults may be able to withstand sarcasm, derision, flippancy, or taunting, but children cannot. Their identities are still shaky, and they do not know how to interpret such attacks. They experience them as overwhelmingly powerful and terribly negating. In some ways they are more devastating than physical blows, which are easier to comprehend and whose effects pass quickly.

Many of my patients have been able to forgive their parents the physical punishment they experienced as children. Fewer are able to let go of humiliations they suffered from derision and mockery.

A forty-year-old airline pilot revealed that his father would make fun of him any time he showed tender or caring feelings:

> I had a little parakeet who would fly onto my shoulder when I came into the room. I used to coo to it and whisper softly to it. How my father mocked me for that. I was only six years old. With disgust in his voice, he used to say "aren't we the little bird?" as he flapped his hands in contempt. I felt so ashamed of myself.

A medical technician in his late twenties recalled:

> Whenever I failed at anything—sports, school, at church activities—my father was not the least understanding. In fact, he'd put me down for it. He'd tell me I was a screw-up and that I didn't live up to the family name. Now I know he was just doing exactly what his father did to him, but at the time I felt like I was a piece of trash. I couldn't even look myself in the mirror.

For their own security children need to cling to their parents' love. But suppose those parents are rejecting and abusive? Since the child cannot afford to be cut off from the object of his affection, he accepts the rejection as correct or deserved. "There must be something terribly wrong with me," he thinks. "Why else would I be treated this way?" The parents' negation is thus taken on by the child in order to continue the illusion of love: "My mother and father are not bad so I must be bad." In effect, the child turns the parents' sadism on himself in order to maintain the primary bond.

The result of accumulated humiliation is to scar the fledgling personality and leave it sensitized to future ridicule. To the child who has been repeatedly demeaned, even minor criticism is an embarrassment. Disapproval produces feelings of shame. Consequently, Everyday Masochists learn to avoid any form of censure. Their behavior is pleasing and appeasing, and they will often sell out their own interests rather than risk rekindling their deep and early feelings of humiliation.

MANIPULATIVE LOVE

Maintaining a tight reign on their children is a preoccupation of masochist-producing parents. One way they do this is by using love manipulatively. When the child meets their expectations, love is supplied in abundance. However, when the child "misbehaves," positive feelings are withdrawn posthaste.

A young furniture maker just out of adolescence explains it this way: "When I follow the program, I'm a wonderful daughter. No one is better. But when I decide things for myself, I'm an ingrate and a spoiled brat."

"Not only did my mother stare dagger-eyed at me when I made decisions she disagreed with," complained a twenty-nine-year-old mother of two, "but she would act as if I injured her. She once actually said she would kill herself if I left college."

A patient of mine revealed that after she had dated a boy her father found objectionable, he directly threatened, "If you do it again, I won't love you anymore."

Most love manipulators are not so direct. A deafening silence, a look of disgust, physical withdrawal, statements of disappointment—these are all subtle ploys that make the same point without fireworks.

Dr. Karl Menninger writes, "To cease to be loved is for the child practically synonymous with ceasing to live." This is why the qualified nature of loving can be so destructive. For the child, love is a necessity of well-being, the cornerstone of positive self-esteem. If a parent expresses disapproval by withdrawing affection, the consequences to the child's sense of self will be grave. It is one thing to disapprove of a particular behavior and quite another to disapprove of the person who shows that behavior.

Parents who give and take their love like cards in a poker game create children who are uncertain of their worth and deeply hurt by the lack of genuine empathy and nurturance. They suffer from low esteem and feel they're never quite good enough, a feeling that remains with them well into adulthood. They find it difficult to trust their abilities fully and are deeply influenced by the expectations of others. They are afraid of rejection and censure. They seem always to be waiting for the other shoe to drop, for their spouse, friend, or lover to find them wanting and then withdraw, just as their parents did at an earlier time.

Like repeated humiliations, manipulative love also stimulates an addiction to low-risk, approval-seeking behavior that ensures approbation. The individual will do almost anything to avoid the pain of love slipping away. Nothing is more catastrophic. But as we have seen, overly compliant behavior compromises the child's needs and desires that are at odds with those of the parents, and, in fact, distances him from his core feelings, which he cannot afford to acknowledge.

Parents who manipulate by withdrawing love are also likely to induce guilt in the process. They communicate to their child that "misbehavior" will irrevocably injure or hurt them. An adapted version of a contemporary joke sharply illustrates the point:

> What's the difference between a hard-boiled mother and a masochist's mother?
>
> The first one threatens, "Eat your breakfast or I'll kill you."
>
> The other one complains, "Eat your breakfast or I'll kill myself."

The point is clear. The mother of the Everyday Masochist claims her child's actions cause her grave injury. In response, the child feels guilty and, to avoid hurting her, responds as expected. What the child doesn't see and what the parent certainly won't admit is that the mother's suicide, depression, or headache—whatever injury is claimed—is not the child's responsibility. The mother doesn't have to react self-destructively to a half-eaten breakfast or to any other "misbehavior" for that matter. She exploits her child's love by using it to control behavior through guilt.

Freud's original belief that masochists turn aggression back on themselves as punishment for sexual feelings toward their parents seems true enough as far as it goes. Masochism is a response to guilt, but not simply guilt over incestuous feelings. Any guilt at all will do as long as there is enough of it. It may be guilt over wanting a parent to die, hating a sibling, surpassing a parent's achievement, or the most common type: guilt induced by the parent as a means of controlling the child's behavior.

FROM THE PARENT'S PERSPECTIVE

Despite the years of clinical training, it was not until I actually became a parent that I recognized the overwhelming demands of child-rearing. To raise a little one with wholly conscious awareness of what he or she is experiencing is one of the most difficult and underrated jobs in our culture. A good parent is attentive, patient, intuitive, flexible, thoughtful, physically nurturing, and loving. The toughest part of it all is that these saintly requirements are demanded twenty-four hours a day.

The difficulties of the job have been offset by better parent education and the growing availability of adjunct services like day care. Yet at the same time, our standards for good child-rearing have risen. Once, all that was required was a little love and the disciplined transmission of values. Now we hear talk of affirming the child's identity, providing a nurturing but not overwhelming physical relationship, accepting and encouraging the expression of feelings, balancing structure with freedom and gratification with frustration. Clearly, child-rearing trends vary from generation to generation and era to era. And pity the parent who is confused by which current wisdom to follow.

Perhaps the hardest thing for parents to manage is responding to the changing developmental needs of their children. The newborn requires a certain degree of attention and direction that would be overwhelming to the two-year-old. The toddler's need for assurance is quite unsuited to the more independent fourth-grader. As the child develops, there is a need and a drive toward greater independence and autonomy. Indeed, the whole process of emotional maturation (and the development of identity) is a struggle toward autonomy away from dependence.

This natural movement is often at odds with the emotions that stir in our hearts as parents. One look at the helplessness of the newborn or the vulnerability of the toddler and our instinct for protectiveness is ignited and thereafter burns brightly. Out of biological necessity we are the guardians of our children's welfare. Out of love we are their caretakers. But our protection and caring can also be smothering. We may be so concerned with ensuring our children's safety that we inhibit curiosity and exploration. Should we risk the possibility of injury so that our child can learn about what is dangerous and test his or her own limits and abilities? Can we gracefully allow our children to pull away from us emotionally, as inevitably they will, to answer the increasingly alluring call of their peer group? These are difficult parental dilemmas.

As one parent confessed, "He's the light of my life. When he leaves home my world will be that much darker. I know I hold onto him too tightly, but can you fault someone for holding onto a treasure?"

These "inherently" opposing tendencies—the child's need to develop an independent identity and the parent's increasing emotional and protective involvement—create the potential for masochism. To some degree the tension between these two forces explains the extent and universality of self-sabotage. Perhaps the predisposition toward masochism is built into the very structure of the child-rearing experience.

Predisposition, of course, is a far cry from inevitability. It takes a certain kind of person to turn this dilemma into an ongoing problem. The love of such parents is possessive and restricting. It is selfish and narrow without generosity or magnanimity. Perhaps it should not be called love at all, for the child is merely a possession, an extension, a tool of the parent.

RAISING THE FOUR EM TYPES

Now that we know the general circumstances that produce Everyday Masochists, we might ask what specific conditions create the four types noted in Chapter 3. How does the pleaser's family system differ from the martyr's? What sort of parents are likely to make a family that produces a perfectionist? The answers to such questions will clarify the types themselves and, perhaps, help us avoid pitfalls in our own child-rearing.

Pleasers

Pleasers come from families where a great deal of emphasis is placed on outward appearances. Good manners and physical attractiveness are stressed. There are demands to be sweet, nice, smiling, and acquiescent. One Everyday Masochist recalled her mother's most common admonition. "Sparkle, sparkle," she urged her daughter, "I don't like to see you when you're not smiling."

Parents of pleasers influence their child's behavior through the withdrawal of approval and love, which are equated. Expressions of disappointment are often employed to manipulate changes in behavior. Parents create a good-bad dichotomy. They communicate the message: "We will love you if you are good, but if you are bad. . . ." The implied threat and the disapproval that follows bad behavior condition the child's compliance. In most cases, obedience eventually comes to be experienced as pleasurable.

From the perspective of the behavioral psychologist, the situation can be described simply. The desire to please, which seems to exist in every child, is selectively rewarded while other behaviors—curiosity and assertion, for example—are not. Over time, the young person becomes so proficient at pleasing (and avoiding disapproval) that she can anticipate her parent's expectations and meet them even if they are never spoken.

Because they receive affection, even if conditionally, pleasers have no strong motivation to rebel or withdraw. The rules of the game are simple: As long as I please my parents, I'll be loved. The arrangement works smoothly until the child expresses needs or preferences that conflict with the parent's. Then problems surface.

In most pleaser-producing households, the young person's material requirements are taken care of. All the outward signs of caring exist. Nevertheless, the situation is not healthy because independent emotional and spiritual needs are sacrificed to the parent's "good child" expectations. The assertion of these needs is seen as illegitimate and selfish. In a way, the child's behavior becomes one-dimensional. She learns to be compliant and sweet but doesn't develop other aspects of herself.

PARENTAL STYLE

- Approval and love are linked
- Only "pleasing" behavior is rewarded

IMPACT ON CHILD

- Is overfocused on parent's expectations
- Feels guilty asserting own needs
- Feels worth is contingent on "pleasing" others

MESSAGE TO CHILD

- "Be a 'good child' or we won't love you."

Martyrs

Martyrs are defeated pleasers. No matter how hard they try to capture their parents' hearts, they always seem to fail. Most of their choices are met with criticism. Their friends are not the "right" friends, their interests are not "appropriate," their clothing is too conservative or too faddish. Attempts at meeting expectations fall short of the mark. They are often blamed for things that have nothing to do with them. Subjected to the chronic dissatisfaction of their parents, they feel like hopeless failures.

Here are what some of my martyr patients report their parents said to them.

> My mother was fond of the phrase, "if it wasn't for you. . . ." She blamed me for a lot that went wrong. I was to blame for her not pursuing a career. It was my fault the family had no money. It was because of me that she and Daddy had fights. The worst of it was I believed

her. I felt ashamed of myself like I was a bad person and a bad daughter.

*   *   *

Once I asked my father if he and mother loved me and he said, "We provide for you, don't we?"

*   *   *

I always thought of my mother as an unhappy person. She was depressed most of the time or she felt very anxious. She used to tell me I was just like her—that I was a sad soul, too, and that I would suffer just as she did. She said these things contemptuously, without the slightest trace of compassion.

*   *   *

I don't know how many times Mother remarked, "I never wanted to have a child," but it was more than I care to remember.

The parents' negation of the child is overwhelming. The child feels angry and unjustly treated but powerless to change the situation. To call her parents' attention to her plight, she exaggerates and nurses her suffering. Since she cannot get the attention and validation she needs, the child settles for the moral victory of knowing she's been wronged. Her martyrdom is a way of validating her experience of mistreatment and defending against feelings of defeat.

Eventually, the child's perception that she cannot win her parent's love leads her to the belief that she doesn't deserve to be loved. In fact, she doesn't deserve to be happy. Although she sees herself as wronged, misunderstood, and unappreciated, deep down she believes that her victimization is justified. She is not worthwhile and is only getting what is coming to her.

For such a scenario to take place, both parents must be negating. If there is a positive and affirming relationship with one parent, the destructive input of the other may be offset. Sometimes a kindly grandparent living in the house can supply some of the child's ego needs, but this is not the usual situation. What is most commonly found in the martyr's background is one negating and one indifferent parent, indifference being a more subtle form of negation.

PARENTAL SCENARIO
- Parents are judgmental and critical

IMPACT ON CHILD
- Feels undeserving and worthless
- Feels powerless to impact situation→martyrdom

MESSAGE TO CHILD
- "You are bad."
- "You are wrong."

Avoiders

Although avoiders sometimes come from families where feelings or their expression were not allowed, the typical household is one in which there is unresolvable conflict or pain. To spare itself grief or to keep distance from a difficult situation, the family denies or downplays the traumatic circumstances. To the child, the lesson is clear. It is better not to acknowledge some things, better still to avoid seeing them in the first place.

Consider these avoider-producing scenarios.

- Both parents are heavy drinkers who deny they have problems with alcohol.
- There is an unspoken war, to which no one will admit, between a parent and an in-law living in the house.

- One child is emotionally disturbed and needs professional help, but the family refuses to recognize the problem.
- The parents are in a continual state of conflict, arguing, cajoling, and lambasting each other, yet the children are told there is nothing wrong.

A child's immediate response to these kinds of situations is confusion. Why is he the only one who sees what is happening? Why doesn't someone else acknowledge the obvious? Why is he being punished for saying what is true? This leads to an "emperor's new clothes" scenario in which the child as truthsayer doubts himself, experiences guilt for his feelings and perceptions, and eventually acquires the blindness of everyone around him. The child learns to protect himself and his family by suppressing what he knows and feels.

PARENTING STYLE

- Ongoing family problems are not recognized
- Feelings or their expression are discouraged

IMPACT ON CHILD

- Experiences guilt and self-doubt for acknowledging feelings and perceptions
- Learns to suppress emotions and develop "social blindness"

MESSAGE TO CHILD

- "Problems are better unseen."
- "Feelings are better unspoken."

The avoider household is a lonely and confusing place in which to grow up. Since feelings and psychological realities are never acknowledged, there is always a certain amount of bewildered distress that undermines the child's sense of security. Avoidance is a way of coping with this dilemma.

Perfectionist

The perfectionist-producing family places great emphasis on performance. What matters is success, winning, and doing and looking one's best. Grades are given undue emphasis; musical achievement or other extracurricular accomplishment is stressed; popularity with peers is expected. Second string is judged valueless. Average is a dirty word. Parents create a success-failure dichotomy; if you're not one you're the other. Perfection is linked with love. While the pleaser faces the threat "be a good child or I won't love you," the perfectionist hears, "I won't love you unless you excel."

This message may not be communicated directly, nor is it fully intended all of the time. But when children consistently receive disapproval and criticism in response to failure (instead of understanding or empathy), they soon learn that if they want to keep their parents' positive regard, they'd better be successful. When success is the only behavior that is so praised, the impact of that message is further magnified.

A lawyer in his mid-fifties used to play tennis in high school. He still remembered how his father refused to talk to him after he lost a match. "He'd just stare at me blankly without saying a word—all the way home."

Many parents of perfectionists are "stage mothers" playing out their failed dreams through their children. Others are fixated on success in their own lives. Still others are seeking to raise their esteem through the accomplishments of their sons and daughters.

The American preoccupation with success and high performance, which some have called the new religion of the eighties, renders this child-rearing scenario acceptable and even desirable. But when performance is a prerequisite to love, that tender emotion becomes conditional and its positive effects are neutralized. The love of perfectionist-making parents is, ironically, second-rate. It gives the child the feeling that unless he performs up to standard, he will be rejected along with all the other nonentities. That situation instills doubt about one's true worth and enough inner pressure to make winning a necessity instead of a choice. And that feels very bad indeed.

PARENTAL STYLE

- Excessive expectation for child's performance

IMPACT ON CHILD

- Feels self-worth is contingent on success
- Fears failure; avoids it at all costs

MESSAGE TO CHILD

- "You will be loved if you are successful."
- "Failure is unacceptable."

Chapter **Nine**

Getting into the Change Frame

To change requires only the lifting of a finger, but on that finger rests the weight of the world.

YIDDISH PROVERB

In the alien shadows of a Death Valley afternoon, I found a dust-covered sign propped up against a mesquite tree. It read: "Don't Waste This Life." Maybe it was the desolate surroundings or the surprise of encountering simple wisdom in this unlikely place, but the words stuck in my mind and gave me cause to wonder. They expressed a sentiment I agreed with but did not live. How easy it is to walk through life in a half sleep, going through the motions without much awareness or deep feeling. Easier still to waste time worrying and second-guessing, dwelling on things that no longer matter and struggling against needless anxiety. A life spent fighting one's inner doubts is a squandered life. Neurosis is a form of impoverishment.

Life is too precious, time is too short to waste on self-defeating patterns that get us nowhere. We needn't stay stuck in our masochism. The past needn't define our future. We *can* make personal change. Granted, it's not easy. It doesn't happen overnight or at the weekend enlightenment seminar in the hotel ballroom. But we can change self-inflicted suffering and self-defeating attitudes.

I have seen many people wipe out the Everyday Masochism in their lives, but I have seen just as many fail to make real change. Four characteristics distinguish the first group from the second: desire, patience, commitment, and, above all, courage—the courage to face yourself squarely, acknowledge your emotional pain, and risk acting in ways that you've always felt you couldn't.

Are you ready to begin the journey? Do you have the willingness to struggle and persevere, what Shakespeare called the "native hue of resolution"? Remember those poignant words in the desert: "Don't waste this life!"

MASOCHISM AND CHANGE

Everyday Masochists are usually the most willing of patients until the time comes to move from thought to action. They are insight collectors, intent on gathering as much knowledge about their psychological processes as possible. Yet when the challenge of actually making changes presents itself, they have great difficulty. Why? Some of their hesitancy is due to the reasons already mentioned. But there is more to it than that.

The problem is in how they have adapted to life. EMs tend to be passive, seeing the world as acting upon them and not the other way around. To change, they must challenge their basic passivity. They must initiate rather than hold back their "natural" inclination. Everyday Masochists are cautious.

They tend to avoid taking risks, particularly in the area of so-cial relations. Their preoccupation with avoiding disapproval severely restricts their freedom of action. Without the con-scious willingness to experiment with new behaviors, they can only go so far.

Along with their caution goes a lack of trust in themselves. They don't believe in their abilities. They question their own opinions and wonder about their motives. Change requires faith that one can carry it off and emerge intact. Self-doubt destroys this faith and makes change truly fearsome.

Finally, the heavy burden of unconscious guilt that Every-day Masochists carry lessens the hunger for change. Feeling culpable means you have no right to make things better. You don't deserve to be happy or satisfied. As one of my patients put it, feeling culpable means "you're supposed to be miser-able. You're supposed to be depressed. Suffering is what makes you who you are."

CONNIE

When Connie first came to see me, she was typical of many Everyday Masochists. Other people rolled over her. She felt incapable of setting limits on her boss and her husband. She overgave to her friends, then resented them afterward. She was self-effacing and riddled with doubt. Her life was going nowhere. At thirty-seven, she was still employed as a tem-porary office worker with minimal wages and no job security or medical benefits.

She was married to a man who disrespected her, often put-ting her down in public and criticizing her in front of her children. She felt dependent on him, and though she recog-nized his abuses, she felt helpless to change things. In truth, she was scared to be out on her own.

Historically, Connie had always depended on men to run

her life. She was disorganized and usually in debt. Her male partners controlled her finances and advised her on how to deal with everyday matters.

Her first marriage had been disastrous. Her husband, a counselor in a drug program she attended as a teenager, was fifteen years her senior. Two years after meeting, while still under treatment, Connie married him and quickly had three children. From that point on things got worse. She had numerous clandestine affairs in the hopes of finding the sympathy and direction she lacked at home. None worked out.

After their divorce (initiated by him) Connie drifted from one relationship to another until she met her second husband, a carbon copy of the first. The same relational patterns reasserted themselves, only this time she began to suffer from phobias and panic attacks. When she got to the point where she could no longer ride public transportation to work, Connie knew she needed professional help. I got an anxious call from her about a week later.

From the outset, her dependency switched to the therapeutic context. She wanted two things: my advice and my approval. When these were not forthcoming, she felt resentful but typically refused to tell me about it. Instead, she expressed her anger passively by coming late, disparaging her progress (and, by implication, the quality of my help), and unfavorably comparing me to a previous therapist whom she had seen for two or three sessions.

The big break came about three months into the therapy. After getting her panic attacks under control, I asked Connie to tell the story of her life in the third person, as if she were speaking about someone else. As she started her narrative, she began weeping with great intensity, experiencing the tragedy of her life as never before. Instead of condemning herself for indulging in self-pity, she began to experience real compassion for her plight. She really hadn't had a chance. Her mother had been an alcoholic, a demanding parent who intruded on both daughters and leaned on them for sympathy in her struggles with her husband. Connie's father, something of a tyrant, had favored her sister, a high school beauty queen. While her sibling could do no wrong, Connie was constantly criticized and demeaned.

Connie's emotional needs were neglected, and she was made to feel undesirable and second-rate. To escape from an impossible situation, she turned to drugs. For the whole time she was in a live-in rehabilitation program, her parents never came to visit her.

All the pain associated with her feelings of being rejected and used surfaced in this and subsequent sessions. Connie began to understand that she had internalized the negative messages directed at her. Though her parents were both dead, their words echoed in her mind. She treated herself much the way they had, demeaning her worth and calling attention to her faults.

Many times in the therapy she wanted to turn back from confronting herself. She feared that if she expressed her real feelings, others would withdraw their love and leave her. She also feared that everything her parents had led her to believe about herself was actually true. An inner search would only corroborate her doubts and expose the ugly truth she did not want to confront.

Yet Connie kept fighting her fears. Each week she reported how she hadn't wanted to come to therapy but had pushed herself to do it. She had countless "good reasons" for missing her appointment: the house had to be cleaned; letters needed writing; she was too tired and run down. But she rejected each excuse by keeping her mind on the end goal: self-acceptance. Recognizing her resistance seemed to help. Just talking about it weakened its hold on her and gave her desire to change more breathing room.

Gradually she began making progress. She kept a daily log of ways she made herself miserable, and this helped her to monitor her inner dialogue (see Torment Inventory, pages 104–7). She learned to challenge her inner critic whenever it sounded off. She began to assert herself with her husband. She found she didn't have to lean on him. She was quite capable of planning a monthly budget or running a household. Her confidence increased. She stood up against her husband's verbal abuses. Instead of redirecting anger back on herself, she expressed it appropriately.

Connie's life started to turn around. She realized that she was not the only person in the world with self-doubt and low self-esteem. Understanding this simple fact lifted her out of her isolation. She commented:

> I was in the drugstore the other day looking for a headache remedy when I realized that two entire rows were filled with pain relievers, sedatives, and sleep remedies. Then I recognized something incredibly obvious that turned my head around. I wasn't the only one with problems. All these pills proved it. Other people had trouble dealing with their lives just as I did. The evidence that I was not alone was all around me. And it somehow made me feel better.

The changes Connie made were hard won and at times painful. But she persevered despite her anxiety and doubt. She was courageous enough to stand up for herself even though she knew it might provoke anger. She acted more independently despite concerns that she would fall flat on her face. She challenged herself and changed her life.

Connie had no inside track on change. She was not more psychologically attuned, brighter, or less pained than anyone else. What distinguished her was the motivation to confront her fears and the determination to try new ways of acting with others. She was tired of Everyday Masochism running her life.

If Connie could do it, so can you. But have no illusions:

Challenging fears is difficult. It is important to move at your own pace. Expect to get knocked down a few times. Expect to regress back into old patterns along the way. But keep going, two steps forward, one back, and soon the changes will come without as much effort. The initial movement—overcoming inertia and the hundreds of excuses that mask your fears—is the hardest.

Once you get by that first barrier, you'll find that risking feels good. Change is exciting, and all the catastrophic expectations that you had imagined have failed to come true. As Macbeth declared, "Present fears are less than horrible imaginings." Indeed, you have not been abandoned. You have not made a fool of yourself. You have not been exposed as a fraud or a phony. And once more, you feel good about yourself. You're living life on your terms: speaking your mind, getting out of your own way, and valuing your own worth.

RULES AND TOOLS

You're on a journey into the blind jungles of the past, the murky waters of the unconscious, the foggy depths of the unknown. An internal journey that calls on you to stay aware, to think, feel, and intuit your way through the darkness.

The goal is self-acceptance. To achieve it, you'll need to give up your inner critic, learn to know and assert your needs and wants, and gain a broader perspective on yourself, one that encompasses the positive as well as the negative.

Taking a trip like this requires some basic guidelines or principles. Like a good compass, they will keep you on track, pointing you in the right direction and helping you discover when you have veered off course. Look over these principles before you begin.

1. *Your fears don't have to control you.* Some fears are functional and reality-based—for instance, it is appropriate to

be afraid in the company of terrorists. But masochistic fears are not well-grounded. They are overblown and irrational, based on catastrophic expectations and exaggerated outcomes. "If I say no, she'll never speak to me again" is a typical example. Such fears are not omnipotent. You can diminish them by staying calm and relaxed and evenly assessing the "real" consequences of an action or attitude. Controlling fears means controlling your mind. The three Rs—reflection, relaxation, and refocusing—provide a good defense against needless and exaggerated worry.

2. *You don't have to feel guilty.* For sociopaths, guilt may be a useful force to prevent antisocial acts, but if you're an Everyday Masochist you already suffer from too much of it. The last thing you need are more of the inflexible demands for perfection, goodness, and generosity that produce deep feelings of wrongness and disappointment in self. By giving up these musterbations you can get the monkey off your back. Guilt is excess baggage. There is nothing redeeming in it.

3. *You don't always have to be liked.* Being liked is not the prerequisite for happiness. On the contrary, it often produces the opposite effect by pushing you to compromise your integrity to gain someone else's affirmation. Life is not a popularity contest. A 100 percent approval rating doesn't guarantee personal fulfillment. Besides, the most respected individuals are not glad-handers or vote-getters but those who follow the dictates of their own hearts and consciences.

4. *You have a right to assert your needs and preferences.* Surviving in the world demands a certain degree of self assertion. There is no reason to condemn it as selfish or egocentric unless it infringes on someone's rights in the process. Knowing what you want (and need) is the cornerstone of satisfaction. Acting to get it is both healthy and reasonable. If you don't assert for yourself, how can you expect others to?

5. *You can forgive yourself for past mistakes.* To make mistakes is human; perfection is an ideal. Dwelling on errors

doesn't earn you points for righteousness or provide exoneration. It only makes you feel worse. Don't be so critical of your frailties. A spirit of conciliation is important and necessary. The best way to deal with failure is to learn from it, not to aggravate yourself about it. Let the past go, but remember its lessons for the future.

6. *You are not the only person in the world with problems.* When you feel isolated, your difficulties loom larger. However, you are not alone. Nearly 50 percent of the subjects in my research showed some masochistic traits. The statistic may not make it easier to change, but it offers this reassurance: Many people know what you're going through and are having similar experiences. You are wrestling with problems that are familiar and universal.

7. *You don't have to meet other people's expectations.* No unspoken life requirement says that you must think or act as others see fit. Enslaving yourself to the demands of parents or lovers is a way of avoiding responsibility for yourself. Trying to please all the people all the time doesn't work anyway. Human beings are not chameleons who can change their exteriors to meet another's agenda. Keep in mind the obvious: Other people's expectations are more in their interest than yours.

8. *You are not hurting others by being all that you can be.* On the contrary, the happier and richer your life, the more likely you are to make your corner of the world a better place. It is dissatisfaction, envy, and enmity that hurt people. Use your talents, develop your natural abilities, extend your limitations, challenge your fears. Your fullness adds to the world; it does not take anything from it.

A GUIDE TO TOOLS

With these eight principles in mind, get ready to begin the journey. Along with those that appear in Chapter 4, the following exercises are tools for the trip. They can be used to bend, shape, and restructure your way of viewing yourself and the world. Like any tools, they must be handled with care and not misused. You can easily defeat yourself with a skeptical or hopeless attitude. Be open to what you discover and let your feelings affect you. Stay alive to your own subtlety. A multitude of sensations inside you are waiting to be experienced.

Tools are only a means to an end; change depends on the person using them. When two people perform the same exercise, one may be overwhelmed with insight while the other wonders what the fuss is all about. The first benefits, the second is left in the dark. The difference? Attitude, of course, but a great deal also depends on the thickness of their armor. Reich used this term to describe the defensive shell we put around our true selves as protection against the world. He was speaking in a figurative as well as a literal sense. When our armor is inflexible, we are less sensitive organisms. We lose accessibility to feelings. Joy is sacrificed to avoid pain. Emotion is thought about, not felt. Don't let your armor get in your way. Be receptive to these exercises and risk feeling happier and unburdened.

The tools are drawn from various psychological orientations. Behavioral interventions sit next to transpersonal techniques; gestalt exercises are juxtaposed against stress reduction procedures. This is not a potpourri, it is a synthesis of the techniques I have found over the years to be most effective in dealing with Everyday Masochism. Some exercises are given as "homework" assignments; others are used in the psychotherapy hour itself. Special tools at the end of the section are designed specifically for each of the four EM types.

I have placed the exercises in the order I believe will have the most impact, but if a particular operation doesn't work for you, feels too upsetting or threatening, move on to the next. People who have a history of emotional disturbance should not undertake these procedures without clearance from their therapist.

ASSERTION AND INITIATION TOOLS

IDENTIFYING WANTS

The refrain goes this way: "If I only knew what I wanted, I could find happiness, but I just don't know!" How many of you are in this boat? And ironically, the greater your freedom of choice, the more confused you are. Choices are based on preferences, preferences on wants, and wants on wishes. The following exercise will help you find a direction for your life by examining your wishes.

Step 1: I am lending you a very special object, an Aladdin's lamp that will allow you to create the world of your dreams. What does your "most wished-for existence" look like? Write about your ideal job, home, intimate relationship, friendships, and so forth. Give your imagination free reign to express itself.

Step 2: Examine what you've written. Are there any surprises? What do your fantasies reveal aout you? About the direction you want your life to take? Look at a particular area, such as work. What are the principal desires expressed? For example, if you wrote, "I want to be president of a company, get a big salary, answer to no one, and spend my time managing people and not papers," we could extract the following: You want a job with authority that is people-oriented, gives you independence, and pays you well.

Step 3: Consider what kind of job might approximate these requirements. Perhaps a profession such as psychology or a job as sales manager for a manufacturing company.

Step 4: Isolate another area. Repeat the same sequence as

above until you have a clearer sense of your preferences. In every case begin with a broad wish, extract its essence, and construct a choice that approximates its essential components. What begins as fanciful thinking can be shaped into realistic possibility.

RISK EXERCISES

Taking risks, particularly interpersonal risks, is very difficult for the Everyday Masochist, who tends to be overcautious and deliberate. These tools are designed to help you become more adventurous and learn that the feared consequences of risk-taking are almost always exaggerated.

The Risk List

Step 1: With paper and pencil in hand, ask yourself: "What sort of interpersonal experiences are most difficult for me?" "Which do I shy away from?" Do you avoid verbal arguments, saying what you really feel, speaking before groups of people? Make a detailed list of all your feared behaviors. Include at least fifteen.

Step 2: Rate each item on the list from 1 to 7 in terms of degree of personal difficulty, 7 being the most troublesome. Divide the behaviors into three groups, those rated 1–3, 4–5, and 6–7.

Step 3: For the next week, take one risk a day from the first group (1–3). If there are not enough risks, repeat one that you've already done. Notice what you feel before, during, and after risk-taking. Was the risk as hard as it seemed beforehand? How did you feel about yourself after taking the risk?

Step 4: In week two, take one risk a day from the second group (4–5). Follow the same instructions as above.

Step 5: In week three, take one risk a day from the third group (6–7).

Step 6: In week four, act on the seven most difficult risks

again. Compare the second time around with the initial experience. Does this comparison tell you anything about the nature of risk-taking? About yourself?

Potpourri

Each day do one of the following:

1. At a store, ask for change of a dollar without buying anything.
2. Confront someone who has been mistreating you.
3. State an opinion of yours that you know is unpopular.
4. Introduce yourself to a perfect stranger.
5. Point out your strengths to someone you feel underestimates you.
6. Tell your boss something that you've been holding back.
7. Take an action that you would rather postpone.
8. Act contrary to all expectations.

When taking these actions, stay aware of your feelings and observe your inner states of mind. If one risk seems more difficult than another, ask yourself what makes it so hard. Be cognizant of how the fear of humiliation and disapproval works into the risk-taking process.

WILL DEVELOPMENT

Everyday Masochists have obstructed wills. They feel incapable of actualizing goals and choices. They don't believe they have the energy, discipline, or ability to control their own destinies. When will is missing, its place is taken up by apprehension, doubt, and confusion. This exercise is a tool to help you reclaim your own will and to recognize that you can direct your own life according to your needs and choices.

Discovering your will is paradoxically simple. You find it by using it.

Step 1: Make a straightforward plan, like going to the

store, and carry it out. Be aware of the role that will plays in the process.

Step 2: Make a plan that involves a minor obstacle and carry it out. Notice your reaction to the obstruction.

Step 3: Make an intricate plan with many obstacles and carry it out. Again, observe your attitude and feelings as you encounter impediments. Do you feel frustrated, defeated, stimulated? Do you feel futile or out of control? If so, redirect your attention to your original intention. What do you hope to gain by carrying out your plan?

Step 4: Break a habit. Bring all your resources to bear. Notice when you start to feel pessimistic, hopeless, or negative. Remember back to your other experiences in this exercise. How did you motivate yourself against hopeless feelings then?

Developing the capacity to actualize goals requires avoiding defeatist feelings from the past, staying in touch with the original motivation, and remaining focused on the goal.

ANGER RELEASE

Everyday Masochists have trouble expressing anger. They store it up and turn it back on themselves or displace it onto the wrong (usually weaker) person. Neither alternative offers a satisfactory resolution. What follows are behavioral interventions to help you feel more comfortable verbalizing your aggressive feelings.

Step 1: Put a chair in front of you to symbolize the particular person who has angered you. Face the chair and report your feelings in a dispassionate tone. What was it about his or her actions, inactions, or attitude that specifically angered you? How long have you felt this way? Why is the issue important? Notice your reticence about expressing these sentiments. Observe whether you are overqualifying your words to avoid an angry response. Is this sort of emotional reporting difficult to do?

Step 2: Now address the person with the same content message as before; this time, however, allow your tone and gestures to express the depth of your feeling. Let your facial expression, posture, and eyes convey your anger. How is this different from the first experience? Is it harder or easier to do? Do you feel out of control, wrong, self-conscious, liberated? Are you holding anything back? What effect does saying what you feel have on your level of anger? Has it dissipated or increased?

Step 3: Write this person a letter expressing the same sentiments you just expressed aloud. Are you more in touch with your feelings? Is the written word as satisfying? Less satisfying? Do you qualify your written words more than your spoken words? Other differences?

Step 4: Arrange to talk to this person. Observe your resistance to doing it. What rationalizations are you using to justify remaining silent? Are you postponing the meeting longer than necessary? During the encounter, notice how the symbolic exercise differs from the real thing. Are you more equivocating, diplomatic, cautious? Keep an eye on whether your gestures and tone are consistent with your feelings. Is it hard to express yourself? If so, what are you most afraid of: rejection, losing control, retaliation?

Step 5: After the experience, notice how you feel. Are you still anxious, relieved, depressed? Did the expected consequences materialize?

Step 6: The day after the encounter, do an awareness check. Do you feel better for having expressed your feelings? Would you do it again? What have you learned about yourself from the experience? What have you learned about your anger?

SETTING LIMITS

Hesitant to set limits on others or on how much of themselves they are willing to give, Everyday Masochists rarely use the word *no* unless it is followed by a lengthy justification (see "Dexifying," pages 87–88). As with the expression of anger, the reasons for this state of affairs are as follows:

1. They are afraid that setting limits will provoke rejection—the loss of love, friendship, or respect.
2. They are afraid that setting limits will provoke anger.
3. They feel guilty for setting limits; they believe they don't have the right.
4. They are afraid of hurting someone's feelings.
5. They are afraid that setting limits implies they are selfish or bad.
6. All of the above.

If any of these reasons apply to you, use the following paper and pencil exercise.

Step 1: List situations and people with whom you are having trouble setting firm limits. Consider all your significant relationships, including your boss, coworkers, spouse, lover, friends, children, and teachers.

Step 2: In every case, consider your motivation. Consult the list above and place a number (or numbers) next to each situation that most closely corresponds to the appropriate motive. Is there a pattern in your choices? What does it suggest? Is setting a limit *really* going to produce the anticipated consequence? Are you giving your fears too much power?

Step 3: What is the price you are paying for failing to set limits? Is the cost worth it? What are your feelings toward the other person? What are your feelings toward yourself?

Step 4: Choose two people or situations from your list each week and set appropriate limits. Be aware of your resistance to this process. Did the catastrophic expectations materialize? How did you feel immediately after setting limits? The next day? What effect did your new behavior have on others? Did repetition make the experience any easier? Continue this process until you have exhausted the list.

GETTING TO KNOW YOUR INNER CRITIC

Yes, of course you know it, but do you *know* it? This exercise brings the critic to life in a new way, giving it shape and form, fleshing it out, making it an entity. Only through this kind of contact can you see how really weak and feeble this vituperative tyrant is, a wizard with a big voice but no power beyond what you give it. Before you begin, familiarize yourself with the operations below. This will allow you to proceed through the nine steps without breaking concentration.

Step 1: Give yourself an hour and find a comfortable, quiet place where you won't be bothered. Lie down on a firm surface with your knees up. Breathe deeply into your abdomen, and for ten minutes follow your breath. Relax. Repeat this phrase to yourself: "At this moment nothing is expected of me." After a few minutes, measure its effect. Now refocus attention on your body. When you feel your back letting down into the mat, move on to the next step.

Step 2: Close your eyes and imagine smoke rising from a cigarette. Watch its progress as it curls lazily into the air. Now let the image go and visualize clouds moving through open sky. Deepen your exhalation as you follow their progress across the horizon.

Step 3: Allow the clouds to fade into the background, and reflect on this thought: All human beings have a core personality, enduring traits that remain constant regardless of the situation, but we also have many subselves acquired in the course of our lives. There is the rebellious self, the altruistic self, the heroic self.

You are now going to summon your critical self, that part of you that chronically finds fault with your actions or attitudes. This is the parental self, always there to tell you what you should do and to point out your failures and shortcomings. We all have this inner critic, but its voice is loudest in the Everyday Masochist.

Step 4: Recall an incident when you felt the heat from your critical self. Remember the details of the situation. What did your inner critic say to you then? Hear its words admonishing you. Listen to the tone of its voice. Is it disgusted, fearful, contemptuous? Does it repeat one or two phrases over and over again? Do its words seem reminiscent of your parents' admonitions? How do they make you feel?

Step 5: Visualize a large, empty, white billboard in your mind's eye. Let an image representing the critic appear on it. Don't push to create an image. Don't think about what it should look like. Instead, allow it to spontaneously emerge before you, effortlessly surfacing from the recesses of your mind. What shape does it take? What color is it? Does it have an animal or human form? Is it large or small? Menacing or friendly?

If nothing appears, don't panic. Using the imagination in this way sometimes requires a little practice. Stay relaxed and take a few more deep breaths. Visualize the back of your hand. Hold it in your mind for as long as you can. Now go back to the critical incident and listen again to the words of your inner critic. Once more allow it to take form on the billboard.

Step 6: Hold the image in your mind. Study it and record it in memory so you can bring it back at will. You may be surprised by your visualization. One patient saw her inner critic as a jagged stone that bludgeoned her into submission. Another imagined his fourth-grade teacher who had bullied him mercilessly for an entire year. Your vision of the critic will have its own character and its own meaning for you.

Step 7: Once you have visualized your personal tyrant, you're halfway home. You've separated yourself from it; it is now outside you. Having achieved this new relationship, you will find that you can see the critic more objectively and control it more easily. But you're not finished yet. Imagine a conversation with a critic. Tell it how you feel about it. Ask it questions. Recall old incidents of oppression. What does it say in return?

Step 8: Now let the image of the critic begin to fade into the background, getting smaller and smaller until it is a tiny dot that finally disappears from the billboard.

Step 9: Do an awareness check. What do you feel in your body? What is your mood? What did you learn about the faultfinding side of yourself? Many people report a sense of lightness after going through this exercise. They experience the objectification of their inner critic as an unburdening, a release.

Finish the exercise by taking three deep cleansing breaths. Share your feelings with someone you trust.

TOOLS FOR RAISING SELF-ESTEEM

The problem is not in your worth or adequacy. Every human being has aptitudes, abilities, and value. The problem is how you were originally taught to see yourself and how that early view is still current. As a matter of fact, you're constantly reinforcing your tarnished self-image by feeding negative information into consciousness and discounting the positive. This creates a no-win situation. No matter how successful you may be, only your faults are acknowledged.

The tools that follow are antidotes to the "screening" process. They will help you achieve a more accurate and balanced picture of yourself. Make them a regular part of your daily routine.

ACTIVE AFFIRMATIONS

Make a space in your schedule every evening to repeat the eight principles at the beginning of the chapter. Say each one to yourself until its meaning registers and you feel agreement in both your mind and body.

SELF STROKES

Each day, record five things you did or didn't do about which you feel positive. These can be of minor significance, such as "I paid my bills on time," or major accomplishments, such as "I stood up for myself with the boss." Also include strokes for not tormenting yourself—for example, "I accepted my friend's criticism without feeling that she didn't like me." The important thing is that you begin to notice ways in which you are successful, competent, and in control of your life.

SUCCESS SCRAPBOOK

Search your memory and write down in a notebook the most significant successes, triumphs, and achievements from all the areas in your life. Give yourself credit where it is due but also be aware of subtle victories, such as taking risks, asserting for preferences, and setting limits. Keep this journal up to date, and consult it whenever you are feeling uncertain of your abilities or doubtful of your adequacy.

JOB INTERVIEW

You're going to be interviewed for the perfect job, the one you've always fantasized about—the interesting one with the generous salary, excellent working conditions, and supportive boss.

Step 1: Write down seven reasons why you, and not someone else, should be hired. Be aware of what you feel during this process. Is it difficult to recognize your virtues? Do you feel any resistance to singing your own praises? If so, what are you afraid might happen? Has it ever happened before?

Step 2: Look over your list. Take each attribute and write four or five more sentences about that particular quality in you. Without embarrassment or skepticism, give yourself permission to openly praise your strengths.

Step 3: Reread what you've just written. Allow the words to affect you; soak them up like sun on a December afternoon. Does this way of seeing yourself feel different or strange? Is it any less accurate than the way you usually view yourself? Does it challenge any preconceptions? Measure its effect on your sense of self.

POSITIVE RECALL

Step 1: Recall an experience in which you showed physical or emotional courage. What enabled you to rise to this specific occasion?

Step 2: Recall an incident in which you challenged a self-imposed limitation. What made this experience different from other less successful challenges?

Step 3: Recall a time when you took a harder path in order to remain true to yourself. What gave you the strength to choose it?

Step 4: Find the pattern in all these experiences. What does that pattern tell you? How does this knowledge affect you?

BODY WORK

Step 1: Write a description of your body that includes only those aspects you dislike. Allow your inner critic the same free reign as when you're giving yourself the once over in front of the mirror.

Step 2: What do you notice about your negative feelings?

Are they deeply embedded? How do they relate to societal messages about the ideal body? Do they reflect any feelings you had about yourself during adolescence? Criticism from Mom and Dad? Comparisons with other men and women? Do the parts of your body you dislike feel less alive? What would happen if you lived more in those parts?

Step 3: What is your fantasy of how your life would be different if you had a more perfect body? How would others relate to you? How would you feel about yourself? How much truth is there in this fantasy? Would your life really be any more satisfying or fulfilling?

Step 4: Write down all the things you like about your body. Was this harder to do than the first description? If so, why? What conclusions do you draw from this?

Step 5: Again describe the negative features of your body, only this time write about them as positive attributes. What is your reaction to this new way of thinking? Do you feel different about yourself? What does it tell you about the lens through which you see your body? Yourself?

GUILT-RELEASING TOOLS

Guilt is an insidious enemy. You're hardly aware of its presence, yet, like an inconspicuous gas that poisons the atmosphere, its effects are powerful and destructive. Though hidden, it is the driving force behind Everyday Masochism.

When guilt is brought out into the open, its impact is sharply diminished. Awareness changes its chemistry and lessens its influence. The first step in dealing with guilt is to expose it. Once that is done, the faulty assumptions that underlie it can be attacked. The exercises that follow are constructed to reveal the workings of this hidden foe. For where guilt is found, so is its by-product: self-punishment.

DEVELOPING COMPASSION FOR YOURSELF

All right, in eighth grade the conductor of your junior high school orchestra singled you out in front of the rest of the kids and told you not to play. It was humiliating, but why do you continue to think about it whenever you hear a symphony? Why is the incident still emotionally charged? For that matter, why won't you forgive yourself for all the other times when you made a stupid error, said the wrong thing, behaved badly, or embarrassed yourself?

Because they lack compassion for themselves, Everyday Masochists are unforgiving of their faults. (Martyrs are this way toward others as well.) They refuse to give themselves a break, mistakenly believing that if they were to forget past humiliations, they would either lose their identity or end up repeating their mistakes. This approach only undermines their self-esteem and further reduces their confidence. They need to treat themselves with more empathy and understanding.

Step 1: Write about an experience of failure in your life. It can be about any costly error, from unrequited love to the time you got fired, but tell it without censuring; allow your inner critic free expression.

Step 2: Wait about fifteen minutes and write the same story as if the experience happened to a close friend you admire and care about.

Step 3: Compare the two versions. Which story contains more reproach and deprecation? Which shows more compassion and sympathy? Which version do you prefer? What do you conclude from this experiment?

Step 4: Rewrite the first story with sympathy and concern for yourself. Note any resistance to this new way of seeing things. What do you experience when you allow compassion in?

FORGIVING YOURSELF

Step 1: List the worst things you have done, said, felt, or thought, things for which you have not really forgiven yourself—for example, the time you turned your back on a friend, ridiculed a helpless person, degraded a lover, assumed a false pride, lied to a holy man. Any of these will do, and the longer the list, the better. Also include ways in which you have disappointed yourself or others.

Step 2: Reflect on every item on the list and allow yourself to feel any regret you might have. Now forgive yourself for each. Speak the words aloud, beginning each response with the phrase "I forgive myself for. . . ."

Step 3: Write down what you've just spoken. Repeat the procedure for three nights. Have you really forgiven yourself? What do you feel? Is there any payoff in maintaining an unforgiving stance?

EXITING THE BLAME GAME

Unless you're a martyr (who faults others as a defense), you blame yourself too much. You take too much responsibility for problems and fail to see everyone else's contribution. The simpleminded castigation that comes with assigning fault helps no one. Blaming oneself creates feelings of guilt and inadequacy. Blaming others produces a sense of powerlessness and victimization in the blamer and defensiveness in the accused.

Preoccupation with fixing blame is an essentially fruitless activity. It keeps you focused on the past and prevents you from changing things for the better. The next exercise is designed to help you stop playing the blame game and move on to more constructive ways of dealing with human error. (A specific "blaming" exercise for martyrs follows later in the chapter.)

Step 1: Write about a problematic situation in your life

that still has an emotional impact on you. Tell the story as if you are completely to blame for everything that happened. Don't distort facts, just select and interpret them to show that you were fully responsible for what occurred.

Step 2: Rewrite the same narrative, ascribing responsibility to all the parties involved. Is this difficult to do? If so, what is your resistance to viewing the situation in this way? Does the rewritten story provoke any new thoughts about your role in the incident? Does it challenge any preconceptions about yourself?

Step 3: Rewrite the story once more without attributing any blame or responsibility. How does the tone of the narrative change? How does the meaning of the story change? What are your feelings about the incident now? Reflect on what is learned by comparing these three versions of the same experience.

TOOLS FOR DEALING WITH OTHERS

You already know how prone you are to Sadomasochist Tangos. You also know how exhausting human relations can be for you. Yet you cannot live in isolation, cut off from the human community. Here are a few operations to help you deal more effectively with others in both your personal and professional lives.

EXPECTATION INVENTORY

Step 1: Just as you created an inventory of "shoulds" (see Chapter 4) to understand the nature of your guilt feelings, it is useful to do the same with expectations. Take a week to examine your life before writing anything down. Then record what you think (and in some cases feel) your parents' expectations are for you. Now list your children's, spouse's, best friend's, boss's, and so on until you have included the expectations of every significant individual in your life. What is your reaction to all these expectations? Does the number surprise you? Do they feel burdensome, uplifting, irrelevant? Which of the expectations do you try to meet? Why these and not the others?

Step 2: Imagine a life lived entirely as you choose to live it, free of the expectations of others. What feelings does that idea evoke? What fears?

Step 3: Each day for the next two weeks, select an expectation from your list and resist your habitual tendency to meet it. What is your reaction to the experience? How does it feel? Did the feared consequences materialize? Which expectations were hardest to surrender? Are there any expectations you weren't willing to give up? A life in which actions are motivated by real interest and heartfelt feelings, not other people's expectations, is within your control. What holds you back from living in this way?

ROLE REVERSAL

Most sadists will resist any change in the power dynamics of a relationship, but if you can get your persecutor partner to participate in this exercise, you may have a chance to make him or her aware of your feelings.

The role reversal is a standard technique used by couple counselors to help people understand their partner's feelings and point of view. The adapted version that follows is designed to show the sadist how it feels to be mistreated, and the masochist how he or she may be provoking abuse.

Step 1: Each partner writes about a recent incident of conflict, from his or her own point of view. Include in the description what happened, what was said, and how you felt.

Step 2: Now write about the same incident from your partner's point of view with special emphasis on his or her feelings. Did you feel any resistance to making the reality shift? Did you learn anything new about your partner's position? What is it like to be in his or her shoes?

Step 3: Exchange second narratives and notice how well your partner captured your perspective. What was left out? What was deemphasized?

Step 4: Share feedback with your partner on the accuracy of his or her perceptions. Don't fight over whose view of the incident is correct. What matters is whether you are able to understand how your partner experienced it.

Step 5: Repeat steps 2 through 4 again. Did feedback improve the accuracy of your second attempt? If not, confront the reasons why. What can you learn about your relationship from this exercise?

QUICKIES

After doing each of the following, measure its effect on you. What did you feel? What did you fear? What did you learn?

1. Allow yourself to receive without giving back.
2. Provoke someone's disapproval.
3. Say "no" without giving any reasons.
4. When you receive a compliment, let yourself feel it and acknowledge appreciation.
5. Don't compare yourself to anyone else for one month.
6. Speak your mind for a day.

SPECIAL TOOLS

The exercises that follow were created to address the specific needs of each masochist type.

MARTYR

Step 1: Write about a situation in which you felt victimized or misunderstood. Focus on how you were wronged and had no responsibility for events as they occurred. Does it feel comfortable or familiar to see things in this way? What emotions are stirred by the story? How do you feel toward your-self?

Step 2: Write another version of the situation, but this time take complete responsibility for everything that happened. Don't distort any basic facts; just select and interpret them to show that you were fully responsible for the flow of events. What is your reaction to the second story? Did you have a hard time writing it? Why? What feelings are elicited by this different point of view? What does the exercise tell you about your perspective on events?

PLEASER

Step 1: Choose a person in your life whom you've tried especially hard to please. Make a list of what you consider this individual's positive qualities; now make a list (equal in length) of negative traits. Which list was easier to compile? Why?

Step 2: In your next interaction with this person, hold yourself back from engaging in pleasing behavior. How does it feel to do this? Anxiety provoking? Awkward? Liberating? If you feel anxious, what is the feared consequence of not pleasing? Now check out what actually happened. Were your expectations met?

Step 3: Relate to the person in a new way. Assume a more equal position, suppressing the temptation to be sweet or nice. What is the effect of this new behavior on the person? On you?

Step 4: Choose another individual and follow the same sequence. Is it easier this time? What do you feel? What conclusions do you draw from these two experiences?

PERFECTIONIST

Step 1: Choose one major area of your life—work, family, friendships, sex, intimate relationships, or play—and list the demands for perfection that you make on yourself. You may have difficulty exposing them at first, so go slowly. Be as specific and forthright as possible. Do you always require high productivity at work, passionate lovemaking in bed, faultless groundstrokes on the tennis court? After you compile the list, ask yourself what would happen if you gave up these demands. Would your lover think you inadequate, the boss fire you, and so on?

Step 2: Experiment with your fears by softening one of your demands. Notice what happens. Does your performance suffer greatly? Does it improve? What feelings are provoked? How do others around you respond? What's the payoff in holding onto impossible expectations?

Step 3: Continue this process, relaxing one demand per week until you have exhausted the list. Measure the effect of each experience on your level of comfort and anxiety. What have you learned?

Step 4: Consider whether you apply the same perfectionist standards to others. What is your reaction when they fail to meet your requirements? How do they react to your reaction? What is the price you pay for maintaining these expectations for your children, spouse, subordinates, friends?

AVOIDERS

Step 1: Keep a journal in which you record situations during the day that make you feel uncomfortable or anxious. Expect some difficulty at first. Here are some clues to watch for:

1. You get a sudden urge for a cigarette.
2. You go to the bathroom with unusual frequency.
3. You "space out."
4. You begin to sweat.
5. You doze off.
6. You get a headache.

7. You get an immediate impulse to eat.
8. You lose your concentration.

Step 2: Look for patterns in your discomfort. When do they occur? What situations precede the above clues? A simple example: "When the boss comes into the office, I start to sweat."

Step 3: What feelings underlie the discomfort? Anger? Fear? Sadness? Hurt? Longing? Enter these in the journal next to the corresponding uncomfortable situations. What is the payoff in suppressing these feelings? What would happen if you allowed yourself the freedom to feel them? What would happen if you expressed them? What consequences do you fear most? What evidence do you have that your fears are grounded in reality?

WHEN TO SEEK PROFESSIONAL HELP

The preceding exercises are helpful in promoting positive change, but they do not work for everyone. Some individuals may need more direct, intense, or specific help. For these people psychotherapy can be an effective aid. Consider professional assistance if any of the following conditions pertain to you:

1. You experience the exercises' behavioral suggestions as too threatening, and you feel you need a slower-paced intervention.
2. The exercises stir up deep feelings that you can't resolve alone.
3. Your masochism is significantly frustrating to you in one or more of the four major life areas—family, relationships, sex, and work—and you need more help than the exercises provide.
4. The exercises call attention to self-defeating patterns that you want to learn more about.

FINAL WORDS

The struggle for personal happiness and self-acceptance has lost some of its appeal in recent years. It is not enough to learn to live in harmony with yourself and the world. Now you are encouraged to get ahead, prosper, and achieve. The goals of the eighties are success, fame, and winning.

Actually, you stand a better chance of reaching those goals if you have a strong psychological foundation and you believe in yourself. Yet were it not linked to success, personal growth for its own sake would still be an admirable and enduring aspiration. To discard it as self-indulgent or passé would be shortsighted indeed.

Do not forget that your problems are mostly of your own making. You can take control of your life if you are willing and courageous enough to risk challenging your self-defeating attitudes and behaviors. Personal change is not a mystery. Abracadabra and boiling cauldrons play no part.

A Sufi tale told by T. V. Ananthanarayanan offers an important perspective:

Many years ago there lived a young man who was growing very dissatisfied with living in his small village. So he went to a sage who lived near the village and said, "Sir, living in this village has no joy for me anymore. I wish to acquire great knowledge and expand the horizons of my mind. Please tell me who the greatest teacher is so I can become his disciple."

"Look for the man who sits under the tree with a shirt tied around his head. He is the one who can teach you," replied the sage.

The young man immediately went looking for his teacher. He traveled far and wide, studied with many a teacher, but his chosen master he could not find. After many years he turned back homeward, tired from his travels. As he neared his village he saw sitting in the woods an old man with a shirt tied on his head like a turban. He was overjoyed by what he saw. With tears in his eyes he went up to him and said, "Great master, I have searched for you for many years and in many lands. I am indeed fortunate to have met you at last! And just outside my home, to which I was returning with a heavy heart since I could not find you anywhere!"

The sage laughed heartily when he heard this and only then did the man realize that the master was none other than the sage from his village.

"Master, why did you send me on this tiresome and long journey?" asked the man in surprise.

"When you came to me years ago you were not ready to learn. Your mind was full of great visions. A man like me from your own village could never have been the great teacher you were looking for. The experiences you have gone through will help you look at me with new eyes."

What you need to live a happier and more satisfying life is already within your grasp. You have only to recognize it and commit your heart and mind to your own transformation.

Notes

Chapter 1
24 "a masochist animal": Theodore Reik,
   Masochism in Sex and Society (New
   York: Farrar, Straus, & Giroux, 1941),
   p. 9.
27 transported masochism: Sigmund
   Freud, "The Economic Problem in
   Masochism," in J. Strachey, ed.,
   *Standard Edition of the Complete
   Works of Freud* (London: Hogarth,
   1968), pp. 157–170.
Chapter 2
37 masochists castigate themselves:
   Wilhelm Reich, *Character Analysis*
   (New York: Touchstone, 1945), p. 241.
Chapter 4
99 Richard Burton remarked: *New York
   Times*, "Therapists Find Many
   Achievers Feel They're Fakes,"
   September 11, 1984, p. C1.
107 coined by psychologist Albert Ellis:
   Albert Ellis, *A Guide to Rational
   Living* (North Hollywood: Wilshire
   Books, 1961).

Chapter 6

142 five different kinds of troubled companies: Manfred Kets de Vries and Danny Miller in *Psychology Today*, "Unstable at the Top," October 1984, p. 27.

162 almost always unsuccessful: Michael Lombardi and Morgan McCall in *Psychology Today*, "The Intolerable Boss," January 1984, pp. 44–48.

Chapter 7

170 linked to particular emotions: Paul Ekman and Wallace Friesen, *Unmasking the Face* (Englewood Cliffs, N.J.: Prentice-Hall, 1975), pp. 23–32.

173 Letting it flow: Alexander Lowen, *The Language of the Body* (New York: Collier, 1971), p. 209.

173 some sort of discharge: Wilhelm Reich, op. cit., p. 246.

174 movement of the facial muscles: Ekman and Friesen, op. cit., p. 10.

177 a recent study: James Schuele and Alan Wisenfeld in *Cognitive Therapy and Research*, "Automatic Response to Self-Critical Thought," April 1983, 7 (2), pp. 189–194.

177 another study: David Jenkins, Curtis Hames, Stephen Zyzanski, Ray Rosenman, and Meyer Friedman in *Psychosomatic Medicine*, "Psychological Traits and Serum Lipids," 1969, 31 (2), pp. 115–128.

Chapter 8

184 "thought or fear": Erich Fromm, *Anatomy of Human Destructiveness*

(New York: Fawcett Crest, 1973), p. 214.

187 "are dirty": Alexander Lowen, *The Language of the Body* (New York: Collier, 1971), p. 222.

189 "ceasing to live": Karl Menninger, A Psychiatrist's World: Selected Papers of Karl Menninger, M.D. (New York: Viking Penguin, 1939), p. 137.

Chapter 9

232 "with new eyes": T. V. Ananthanarayanan, *Learning Through Yoga* (Madras, India: Krisnamacharya Yoga Mandiram, 1983), pp. 35–36.

About the Author

David Brandt, Ph.D., the author of *Is That All There Is?*, is a clinical psychologist in practice in San Francisco. He teaches at the California School of Professional Psychology and has been a visiting lecturer for the Department of Psychiatry, University of California Medical School, San Francisco. Dr. Brandt and his wife, Laurie, a psychotherapist, live by the ocean north of San Francisco, California.